Love
Style

I Love Style

Simple Tips To Create A Home You Love

JULIET LOVE

NEW HOLLAND

Contents

Chapter 1

INTRODUCTION

I am going to make everything around me beautiful. That will be my life.

The late Elsie de Wolfe, the first lady of interior decoration

Welcome to your dream home

I've always said that walking into a beautifully decorated room can have a profoundly positive impact on your life. A well-designed space should speak to you – it should be inviting, inspiring and make an impact. The magic ingredients for a striking design are intangible, and the secret to a fabulous space is not one thing alone. It's not one piece of furniture, it's not one pattern in a fabric, it's not the flowers on your table. It's a combination of elements that make for a happy home that tells a story.

If a room's décor is executed in the right way, it can literally take your breath away. Imagine experiencing that feeling every day as you walk through your own front door. Just as a brand new frock puts a spring in your step, making you feel vibrant and confident, a makeover for your home will do exactly the same for you. In a few simple steps your home can feel like new. But this book is not just about designing your home, it's about the positive repercussions it can have on the rest of your life – enhancing your happiness with a home that you are proud of, and one that you enjoy spending time in.

Your home should be a sanctuary. It should be a place to rest and recharge, in which you are surrounded by the things that you love. A home is very telling about its occupants – the pride you take in its appearance – even seemingly small details such as whether you brighten your home with fresh flowers, or have pretty hand soap canisters in the bathrooms. Your home is a reflection of your own life and style. The detail is what gives your home its overall impression.

Even for the most uncreative and un-inventive among us, it's possible to create a dream home without the help of a professional. You just need to find your inspiration and approach the project of decorating your home in a methodical fashion. The best interiors are those that are both beautiful, as well as functional. By building up 'layers' in your home you will create interest and warmth.

I was born with an innate love of style and a keen eye for design, and was fortunate enough to land my first job and hone my skills at *Vogue Living*. An incredible experience, my years there taught me invaluable lessons about style and design.

Since my *Vogue* days, I have worked on lots of exciting, fun and creative projects for fabulous clients including Christian Dior, The LifeStyle Channel, EDIT – an innovative furniture and homewares company with the tagline 'Decoration Without Explanation', national property developer, Mirvac, as well as styling and writing work for the print media such as *Home Beautiful, Woman's Day*, and my national column for *News Limited* magazines and newspapers.

One of my favorite jobs was styling the set for *The Morning Show* at Channel 7 as I love television media and also love the show itself. I also presented a series on the same show called 'Amazing Homes' in which I filmed inside multi-million dollar properties that had serious wow factor. It was a tough gig, but as they say, someone had to do it!

Prior to this I co-hosted a show on The LifeStyle Channel called *The Party Garden*, where I met my now husband, landscape designer and television presenter, Charlie Albone. Together we created beautiful outdoor spaces with various homeowners, and threw a big party at the end of each episode.

At times challenging, each job required a completely different approach and an array of design solutions to make the space work for its occupants. I have learnt something from them all and love to impart to others the things I've found out about creating beautiful interior spaces along the way.

With this book, I will pass on to you what I've learnt, and take you through each necessary (and fun) step to create your most stylish home.

You might say my love of style has been passed down through the generations. My late maternal grandmother, Mollie McSweeney, was a supremely stylish woman. In turn, my mother also inherited this sense of style and has had a very successful career based around fashion – from modeling internationally, to interior design, to fashion PR. Both women have, without doubt, inspired me to create beauty around me, and to take pride in my home and my personal appearance.

My grandmother owned a beautiful boutique florist shop in her younger years, and for the remainder of her life would always have freshly cut blooms from her garden

BATHROOM

n
be

H
+ ga

Lau
Bus
In A
To
60-PAGE SPEC

DESIGN ST
REVEAL T
FAVOURIT

All
fas
sp

Stylish steals
Take-home inspiration
from the Crawford's
new boutique hotel p120
ALL HAIL MARSEILLES
The 2013 European
Capital of Culture p119

$9.95

DESIGN ART ARCHITECTURE INTERIORS DECORATING

LIVIN

The art of
mixing past
& present

LIVING

most
amazing
beachside
apartment

SPRING
BLISS

SENSATIONAL
ACCESSORIES TO TRANSFORM ROOMS
DESIGNER WALLPAPERS, FABRICS & FURNISHINGS
FOR THE NEW SEASON

STATE-BY-STATE SHOPP

RENOVATING DECORATING

scattered around the house in dainty vessels of various shapes and sizes. Dramatic wallpaper, stylish decorative accessories and fresh blooms became her signature style at home. Jaws still drop when people walk through her home today, which remains in its original condition and is often used in photo shoots for high-end magazines and in films.

My mother also studied interior design, and as a child I vividly remember how glamorous and beautiful our homes always were. I loved examining the texture and color in the flocked Florence Broadhurst wallpaper and getting lost in the bright lights of the glamorous chandeliers. The lesson I learnt is that to have a beautiful home is happy-making!

Each of us has within us the power to create our own signature style at home that makes us endlessly happy. I hope that with this book, you can find yours.

An interior is the natural projection of the soul.

...

Coco Chanel

Chapter 2

Find Inspiration And Define Your Style

Style is something each of us already has;
all we need to do is find it.

Diane von Furstenberg

Where to find inspiration

Inspiration is everywhere. Even if you feel that you don't have a creative bone in your body, don't despair. The art of style can be learnt.

Magazines

The most creative people find inspiration in everything, so take your cue from them. A good starting point to find a visual direction for your home makeover is in interiors magazines. There are a multitude of incredible images online too, but I have found this to be overwhelming for some clients. I generally ask people to pull tear sheets from key interiors magazines as a launching pad to find their likes and dislikes. Often the dislikes can be the most telling, so don't disregard the things that you find unbearable. They will help you define exactly what you *do* like. Magazines such as *Architectural Digest, UK House and Garden, and US Elle Décor* are my favorites. Even the advertisements are beautiful and a source of creative stimulus.

Books, films and fashion

These sources of style are hugely inspirational. Top set designers and creative directors have made classic Hollywood movies such as *Breakfast at Tiffany's, Auntie Mame,* and all of the James Bond movies a visual feast too. More recent standouts have been films such as Baz Luhrmann's remake of *The Great Gatsby*, as well as the stunning house in the film *Something's Gotta Give.*

Travel

You can't beat exotic locations for inspiration too – different cultures can open your eyes to a whole new world of artistic possibility. A cosmopolitan look can be created by mixing together hints of visual stimuli from different cultures around the globe – French and Moroccan influences, for example, look fabulous when coupled together.

Classical architecture is known for its excellent scale and proportion. Witnessing this first hand on your travels will help you apply it when you get home.

Pinterest

A virtual pinboard, Pinterest is a genius way to find, save and share images that can help you to realize your design. The vast collection of images available, pinned by other members, can provide just the inspiration you need. You can label your boards and create categories for various areas of your home such as the kitchen or bathroom. They also have a brilliant search engine meaning that if you type in the style you are looking for, hundreds of images will come up, directing you one step closer to your dream home.

Nature

Scenes from nature are endlessly beautiful and can provide the help you need – the colors you see in nature are often the best combinations. Mother Nature just knows how to get it right. Pink camellias against a glossy deep green leaf, the blue of the ocean against natural stone rocks, or an apricot bird with tones of brown, peach and white in its feathers are all examples of how nature never gets it wrong with color.

Treasured personal items

Another source of inspiration can be treasured personal items. Cherished family heirlooms, a favorite dress or pair of shoes, or a flower that reminds you of a happy time – these are the things that can become the starting point for your journey to styling the house of your dreams. I once had a pair of highly textural barramundi skin shoes that became the inspiration for a whole room. They were so unique and exciting, and this infused into the whole room. The sky is the limit when you start to identify the things you love most as items of inspiration.

Fabric and wallpaper swatches

Fabric swatches are also a great place to start. Go to a big soft furnishing showroom and take your time looking around. Most companies will usually be happy to provide small cuttings of your favorite fabrics so that you can take them with you and add them to your collection. A lot of online retailers will offer the same service so you don't even have to leave your desk. The same applies for wallpaper samples.

Furniture

If you find a of furniture that you love, you can use it to inspire the rest of your design. For example, if you are designing a children's nursery and you find a gorgeous pale green chest of drawers that can double as a change table, then that can provide the foundation for the rest of the room. You might pick up on the tones in the green paint of the chest in other items such as curtains, or use an array of complementary pastel colors in your color scheme, using the green of the chest to anchor the look.

Stylish people

People whose style you admire are also a great source of inspiration. Be it friends, or those in the public eye, other people can provide a wealth of ideas. Celebrities have the money to hire the best interior designers in the world, and often they allow cameras into their homes to photograph them. Use these images as inspiration to get a similar look.

If you admire the style of a friend or associate, tell them. They'll most likely be flattered and may offer you some advice, if you ask. Mostly they won't have been born with the style they have today and will be willing to share the lessons they've learnt along the way. Mentors are a great way to learn and define your own style.

Architectural periods or styles

Often you can find inspiration in a certain distinctive period or style that you love, and take your lead from there. You may love classic Greek columns, the simplified and elegant style of Hamptons' architecture or early twentieth-century modernist styles. Study images from the period and use whatever features you love most in your own home.

You don't have to be born with style, it *can* be studied. Develop your 'eye' and hone your skills, and you will end up with a beautiful home. Your home should be an expression of who you are, so the best approach is to surround yourself with the things that you love.

Many people have a lack of confidence and subsequent anxiety around decorating their own home. By breaking the exercise down into steps using the practical approach in this book, any fears you have about your ability to decorate should quickly disappear. With each step complete your confidence should grow, until you finish with a home that is bursting with style.

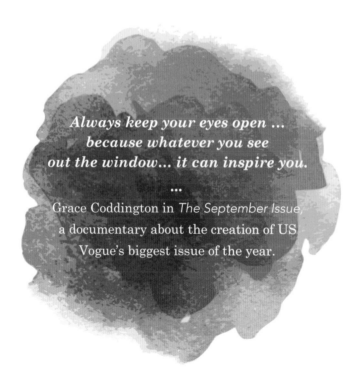

Always keep your eyes open ...
because whatever you see
out the window... it can inspire you.

...

Grace Coddington in *The September Issue,*
a documentary about the creation of US
Vogue's biggest issue of the year.

Canary yellow, mint and navy cushions
in varying patterns and textures for interest

Geometric grey rug

Round clear glass coffee table with modern metal legs

Decorative accessories to create
fresh, new, inviting feel

How to create a mood board

Once you've worked our where your inspiration is coming from, create a mission statement that you can return to when you need some guidance. Just a few words about how you want your home to look will be sufficient. If you have trouble narrowing this down to a few words, carry a notebook with you for a few days, and write down a few words every time you feel inspired. Consider words such as – fresh, vibrant, classic, contemporary, polished, streamlined, boho, or rustic. Elements of anything that catch your eye that you like can help too – silver, metal, leaves, soft, neutral, clear, colorful or happy.

Think about how you want your home to look. What do you want it to express about you? Perhaps more importantly, how do you want your home to feel?

Fashions fade, style is eternal.

Yves Saint Laurent

BIRTHDAY CANDLE

LA VIE EN ROSE

MULBERRY STAIN

POISON BERRY

Creativity takes courage.

Matisse

Now that you have your mission statement, start collecting pages from magazines and other sources (tear sheets), fabrics you love, loved items and other images. With these, you can start a folder or a visual board. These will make up your mood board. A basic, old-fashioned corkboard will do just fine for this purpose. It's a great way to gather your thoughts and start to make sense of things.

You could also use a large piece of cardboard, foam core board, or make a digital version on the computer with desktop publishing software. Include all of the elements that fit with your design including fabric swatches, small tile samples, images, ribbons, words, paint chips – anything that ties your theme together and gives life to your project.

To capture inspiration as it strikes, carry a camera (or your smartphone) with you wherever you go. This is a great way to record what you love so you don't forget it, and you can include the images on your board. A hotel lobby that you love, the interior paint scheme of your favorite café, a house that you drive past and wish was yours, or simply the colors you see in nature on a walk around your neighborhood can all be snapped and used later as inspiration.

Be creative about how you display the items too. Raise selected elements on a piece of foam core board (from art supply stores), roll your fabric swatches, layer paint swatches with artistically folded fabric swatches, and add words that identify the look that you are going for.

Go through your new collection several times and eliminate the items that are not your absolute favorites. You should start to see a pattern or theme emerging.

Certain colors, a minimalist look, a more classic look, lots of distressed finishes, or mostly natural elements such as stone and timber should start to jump out, directing you to a particular style that will then form the basis for most of your future decisions and purchases.

How to narrow and edit choices

If you find that the looks you have chosen are completely different styles, that's ok. You can either narrow down your favorite look or go for an eclectic look. This is easier said than done so I would avoid this look unless you have experience decorating with different styles.

The list of architectural and decorative styles is abundant, which can be overwhelming. By narrowing down your favorite things, you will be able to move forward more clearly, and with more success.

Think like an editor of a magazine. You can't have everything on every page. You can only have the best. So be ruthless, and you'll end up with a better overall look that will help to define your style whether that be classic, contemporary, bohemian, country, or any other of the myriad styles available.

The worst rooms are the ones that are void of personality. Cold and characterless rooms that look like they are copied straight from a high street furniture chain catalogue are uninspiring. So take a chance and allow your individuality to show.

By cutting down your options and making careful design decisions, you can create a home that lifts your spirits.

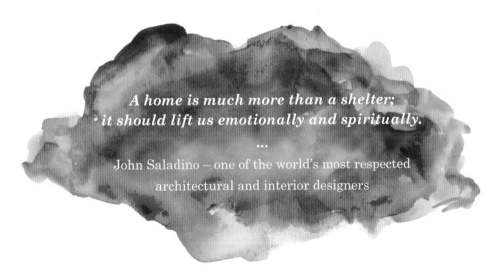

A home is much more than a shelter;
it should lift us emotionally and spiritually.

...

John Saladino – one of the world's most respected
architectural and interior designers

Chapter 3

PLACEMENT, SPACE AND THE PRINCIPLES OF GOOD DESIGN

Happiness is not a matter of intensity, but of balance, order, rhythm and harmony.

Thomas Merton, American writer and poet.

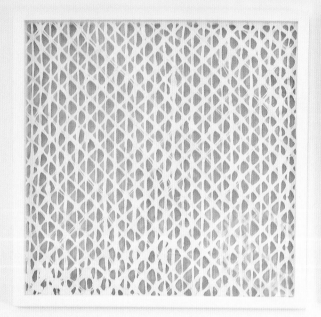
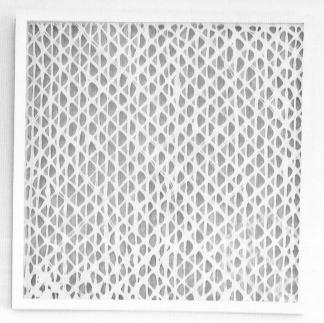

TIME TO DRINK
CHAMPAGNE
AND DANCE ON THE TABLE

Balance and harmony

Particular sets of 'rules' exist around good interior design. As with most rules, some can certainly be broken. However, for the purpose of achieving the best result at home without an interior decorator, the universal principles of design will guide you.

Interior design is all about making a three-dimensional space visually appealing and comfortable. By applying the principles of design, you are much more likely to have a successful outcome.

When designing a house, it's best to work holistically – linking spaces together to create a fluid aesthetic and approach.

Balance is especially important and revolves around the equal distribution of weight in a room. If one item of furniture in the room is much larger than the rest, this can throw the balance out. Similarly, too much pattern in one area, or too many colors being too close can throw out the balance in the room. An imbalance is obvious when the room just doesn't feel visually 'right'. Balance can be either symmetrical or asymmetrical.

Symmetry is where one side of a vertical axis is a mirror image of the other side.

Asymmetry is where dissimilar objects of a similar weight are positioned each side of a vertical axis. There is still visual harmony, but not perfect symmetry. Asymmetry is harder to achieve, but results in a visually more interesting outcome.

A great tool to overcome issues of balance in a room is to take a photo of the room and divide it into four by placing a cross in the middle (that is, a line down each axis). It should become immediately obvious where items need to be added or taken away.

There should also be a **focal point** in a room, where your eye rests on one particular component after surveying the room in its entirety. A striking artwork, a fireplace, or a decorator item such as an unusual lamp, vase or light fitting are good examples of points of emphasis in a room. Oversized flat screen televisions have become popular additions to homes recently, however, these should not be the focal point in a room as they are not a stylish feature! Where possible, television screens and other equipment should be concealed behind a cabinet. Some new televisions are framed and have a special surface to make them look like a mirror when they are not in use which makes for a more designed look.

You also want to avoid competing focal points, such as a busy wallpaper alongside a dramatic artwork, in a room with a strongly patterned rug. There will just be too much competing for your attention.

Proportion is often discussed in relation to the human body – dressing in a particular way can enhance a figure, and the same goes for a room. The right sized objects in a room make for a much more appealing space. If pieces of furniture are in proportion to each other and to the scale of the room, it aids the eye. A room is visually more appealing if the objects in that room are in a scale that is harmonious.

Rhythm is an important principle of design, and most often refers to a repetition of an element that draws the eye and creates a cohesive look. Repetition usually occurs in decorative elements such as pattern, texture, line or color, and helps bring a cohesive feel to the space.

Progression is a group of similar elements going from small to large, or large to small, such as nesting tables or a cluster of candles on a mantelpiece.

Transition is where your eye is naturally guided from one element to the next, usually through architectural features.

Contrast is using items of different color weights to create interest. It is an important element if you want to establish a strong look that is outside of the ordinary.

Placement of accessories on flat surfaces such as on mantelpieces generally look best in **odd numbers**, usually three or five. Avoid spacing the items evenly – if you have three items, place two close together to one side, with the last one a distance away. If you are displaying only one item, it will usually look best slightly off-kilter.

Aspects and functional requirements

The aspect of any home has a significant influence on its feel. The **direction the house faces in relation to the sun** is very important as this determines how much light enters the home.

The size of windows will also dictate how much light enters your home, so you may want to consider having larger windows fitted, or new ones added on the sunny sides of your home.

If your home seems dark and lacks natural light, you can install a sunlight that will allow light to enter through the roof. The designs available now are unobtrusive and cleverly contain a reflective insert that will project the maximum available illumination down into the room below. They are also relatively inexpensive and easy to install (by a professional), and are big on impact. There are small tube skylights available that are low-cost, however, they generally look like utility items so may be a false economy. For this reason, they should be avoided.

Along with the aspect of your home, you need to consider your lifestyle requirements, and what your priorities are for your home.

Interior design is making the best possible use of the available space.

...

Staffan Tolgård, Interior Designer

Spatial awareness and drawing up basic floor plans

Before you embark on decorating any room, you need to be aware of its perimeters, as **the shape and size of a room** will determine what you can do with it.

A tape measure, large format blank paper and a felt-tipped pen are all you need to gauge the space you have to work with to design your new room. Measure the room then draw it to scale. Make several copies and play around with the furniture placement within the space. This will really help you to visualize the room once it's finished.

If you have professional floor plans of your home available, use them to trace the room plan you are working on. You may have to enlarge it on a copier a few times to be able to get a good size to work with. It doesn't have to be to exact. You just need to be able to use it as a tool to help plan different approaches to the room's design and the placement of items. However, if you are able to draw a room plan to scale, you will end up with a more accurate result. You may want to include floor to ceiling built-in cabinetry in your new room, for example, rather than a couple of cumbersome old sideboards. Floor plans showing different options will help you to see how the space works best.

Alternatively, there are many apps available that will help you to generate modern digital projections of your room. You will need the measurements of the room to do this. Some apps even generate 3D drawings for you, which is ideal for those with little experience of visualizing unfinished spaces.

Once you have the floor plan, you can set about working on placement of furniture. The plan will help you decide what size furniture to buy, and also what items of existing furniture will fit. It is also important to consider traffic flow, or ease of movement around the room, and a plan will help to ensure that you have adequate passages between furnishings to move around.

Don't fall into the trap of placing all of your furniture up against walls. Sometimes, bringing furniture in, even just a few inches can make a room feel much more homely and will create a 'zone' that allows for specific use of the space.

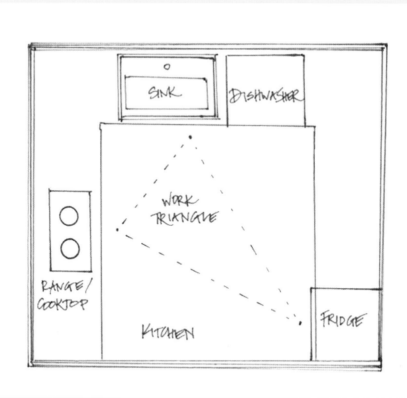

SINK

DISHWASHER

WORK
TRIANGLE

RANGE/
COOKTOP

KITCHEN

FRIDGE

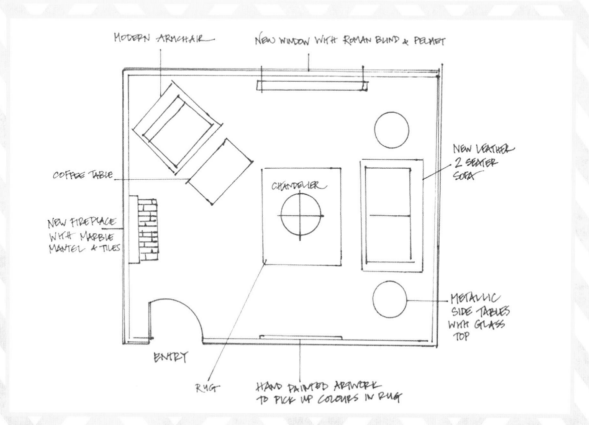

MODERN ARMCHAIR

NEW WINDOW WITH ROMAN BLIND & PELMET

COFFEE TABLE

NEW LEATHER
2 SEATER
SOFA

CHANDELIER

NEW FIREPLACE
WITH MARBLE
MANTEL & TILES

METALLIC
SIDE TABLES
WITH GLASS
TOP

ENTRY

RUG

HAND PAINTED ARTWORK
TO PICK UP COLOURS IN RUG

Chapter 4

BUDGET

A budget is telling your money where to go rather than wondering where it went.

Dave Ramsey, finance expert

How to get maximum bang for your buck

For many people who want to transform their living spaces, renovating or redecorating is an especially stressful time. Setting a budget when you embark on the interior design of your home is an integral part of the project to avoid some of the stress.

To have an effective budget in place at the start of your work, you need to **detail and estimate every expense**. Start by breaking down the costs into categories. For example, you might wish to buy new furniture, materials, window treatments, soft furnishings, flooring, or you may know that a specific job will incur labor costs, repair costs, professional advice and delivery fees. Within these categories, there may be further sub-categories, for example, under materials you might include the cost of paint as well as new tiles. Under labor costs, you may have listed the painter's and tiler's fees. If you are attempting to complete the project yourself, it's fundamental to **include every cost.**

Overspending is a huge issue for home renovators so the importance of setting a budget cannot be underestimated. Many people get trapped when they don't include every detail such as nails, screws and filler. These might seem trivial at the start of a project, but they very quickly add up and can blow the budget. I've seen clients attempt to maintain a budget with scribbled figures on scrunched up note paper, which they keep in their pocket. I would advise that the most effective way to manage a budget is with a computerized **spreadsheet**. Use whatever computer program you are comfortable with. You just need a basic table with headings, sub-categories and most importantly, the figures. If you're not good with numbers, there are some fantastic apps available for your smart phone or tablet that will simplify this exercise for you.

When preparing a budget don't try to spread the amount you have to spend across all the things you have to purchase or you'll come up short. Work out the big picture first and then trim out the things you can live without. As you progress through your decorating project, you need to itemize and list every expense against your estimate as the money is spent.

The best way to do this is by having two columns on your spreadsheet – **estimates and actual costs**. This way you can keep track of your total spend to prevent spending from getting out of hand.

It's wise to do your research, as often you can save a fortune simply by looking for the best bargains. Scour markets for secondhand furniture that can be given a makeover, and look online for the best deals. Auction houses frequently have fantastic deals on kitchen cabinetry, bathroom fittings, and furniture.

It's a good idea to **get several quotes** from any trade professionals you need before you start so that you get the best value for your dollar. If you get a written quote, then the laborer is obliged to stick to that, which is reassuring. Most quotes are made up of material and labor costs.

You should also add 10–15 per cent contingency fund to your estimated spend as there will inevitably be some **unforeseen expenses** in most home renovating exercises, especially in older homes. You might pull down a wall only to find that you have a termite problem, which requires thousands of dollars that you hadn't budgeted for to remedy the problem.

Stick to a time schedule

The other element that can affect your budget is the **timeline**. If a project has a deadline that gets extended several times due to tradesmen taking longer than expected or encountering issues that cost time or money to resolve then this can have a substantial impact on costs.

Some costs cannot be avoided, however, a lot can be circumvented if you manage the project effectively and keep your eye on the ball throughout the entire process.

Key tricks to creating a professional designer look on a budget

You don't have to spend a fortune to get a designer look in your home; you just have to be clever about where you spend your money.

Firstly, you need to strip your home back to its bare bones. It's much easier to see the potential of a room with a blank canvas, especially if you have lived in your home for some time and need to see the room through fresh eyes. You can gain an entirely new perspective on your home when it is uncluttered and you should see your home in a whole new light.

Have one or two showstoppers

It's true you don't have to spend a lot of money on every piece in the room, but you should consider investing in one or two items. If everything is cheap, then quite frankly everything is going to *look* cheap.

The showstopper doesn't have to be a piece of furniture – it would be equally effective to have an upscale Italian light fitting in the middle of your room as a dramatic piece of furniture.

Decorative moldings and architectural hardware

Adding paneling to sections of a wall, usually the lower area, or adding crown moldings to ceilings or walls, will give your space a designer look. Paint them a contrasting color for the most striking effect. You can get easy-to-apply moldings for mass-produced furniture from inexpensive chain stores. When painted they may be transformed into an unrecognizable design piece.

New knobs and handles on cupboards and drawers in kitchens, bathrooms and even on bedroom furniture can be just the update your existing items need. Go for glass or colored knobs, or contemporary silver for a more modern look.

Similarly, new light switches will give your home a designer edge.

Paint

Paint is like a magic wand that instantly transforms interiors from dull to dazzling, from old fashioned to 'oh wow!'

With advances in technology, paint is manufactured now that can be applied to most surfaces including tiles, cupboards such as kitchen cupboards. They will all take on new life with paint.

Rather than opting for the safer neutral look, don't be afraid to try color and different finishes – glossy trims and ceiling paint can make a room instantly feel special.

Using lacquer paint on a vintage piece of furniture can make it instantly chic and designer-like. The glossy finish will transform the item, making it feel unique and brand new.

Designer tip: While the new paints are made to adhere to most surfaces, it is important to prepare the item that the new paint is to be applied to beforehand. To get a smooth finish and avoid the paint looking too thick, a quick rub with some sandpaper will do the trick. Freshly painted walls will also brighten up a tired interior space.

Window treatments

One of the quickest ways to update a room is to change the window treatment. Heavy, dated, and old curtains that have collected dust for years can be removed and replaced with more modern shutters or blinds that will allow more light into the room and look far more fashionable.

Wide slat blinds or French-style shutters are one of the most stylish and contemporary window treatment options. These are now available in ready-made sizes that will fit most standard windows. You will need to be handy with a drill to fit them, but once up, they instantly add a modern feel, and will also allow you to adjust the amount of light entering the room.

If your budget allows, it's worth getting a professional in to advise you on the various options for window treatments. The window frame and hanging options – the type of blind or curtain itself – will make a huge difference to the look of your room.

Design is not just what it looks like.
Design is how it works.

...

Steve Jobs

Cushions

Decorative and practical accessories such as throw/scatter cushions are a great way to introduce pattern or color into your interior without spending a fortune. They are fun, and will provide an instant wow factor. The marketplace is full of retailers offering the latest trends in fabrics, textures and colors, so changing your cushions is one of the easiest and most affordable ways to update the look of your living room or bedroom. They also don't require any work such as hammering or drilling, which is very appealing to most home renovators!

Mix the sizes and shapes of your cushions for the most stylish look. Don't overdo it though. You don't want a sofa that is so full of cushions that you have to perch on the edge.

There are a few general rules of thumb for cushion placement. For a generous two seater sofa, place an oversized cushion (say 24 inch/60 cm square) at each end, and then have an additional smaller rectangular cushion (16 x 8 inch/40 x 20 cm) at one end. The larger cushions could be the same fabric, with the smaller one a complementary pattern and shade. If they are all the same you're at risk of a dreary sofa. This placement relies on the principles of balance and harmony.

Designer tip: Knife-edge cushions
Plush feather-filled cushions look fabulous if you plump them up, place them on the chair or sofa, then hold your hand out straight and place it in the middle of the top edge of the cushion and push down in one swift movement, so that the middle of the cushion is now lower than the two edges, which should form crisp points. This is called 'dog earing' or 'knife edging' and is a very fashionable look.

Light fittings

Lighting is so important in a home as it helps to set the mood and tone. Dated and old fashioned light fittings are a giveaway of the age of your home. Major hardware stores or lighting warehouses sell affordable, contemporary lighting that will create a modern feel in an instant.

To get a designer look, be daring and go for a dramatic metallic finish in your lighting, or an embellished piece such as a chandelier.

Lamps usually look best if they are oversized and have a striking base. If the base is a strong shape, go for a simple, chic shade, and vice versa.

Using lights to highlight artworks or décor will also give your home a designer feel as they are reminiscent of being in an upmarket gallery. You'll read more about lighting in Chapter 6.

The detail – accessories and embellishments

One thing that most professionally designed homes will have is an attention to detail through embellishments such as piping, fringes, or edging on upholstery, pelmets on window frames, and decorative accents thoughtfully placed around the room to tell a story and bring the room to life. Think about adding a contrasting edge to your lampshades or curtains, or a distinctive piped border to your sofa to get a stylish look.

Invest in good quality fabrics

Not unlike clothing, cheap interior soft furnishings are an obvious sign that you haven't spent much on your décor. You can get away with an affordable synthetic sofa, but invest in some good quality, large cushions with designer details such as a piped edge and you'll end up transforming your bargain basement sofa into a head turning designer piece.

Buy vintage

Often vintage furniture can be more affordable than antiques, but just as gorgeous. By spending time scouring flea markets, garage sales or auction houses, you could find a gem that looks like a rare, timeless piece with a big price tag, but for a fraction of the cost.

Add legs

It might sound strange, but elevating your furniture off the floor can give it that designer edge you are looking for. Add legs to the base of an ottoman or chest of drawers and it will instantly look more upmarket.

Expensive accessories

A real silver tray on an inexpensive coffee table can raise it up to a new level of sophistication. Similarly, a designer décor item such as a cashmere throw rug draped across an armchair will make the chair itself seem more glamorous and expensive.

Hang art

A common feature of expensive homes is the art that decorates the walls. The [art?] itself doesn't have to be extravagant, the trick is to hang it like you would see [in a?] gallery – in multiple matching frames, or have one oversized artwork on a main wall.

Save money with eco-friendly cleaner

Beautiful homes look their best when they're clean so save money, the environment, and your health with an eco-friendly, super cheap multi-purpose household cleaner.

I've been using my own homemade version for the past five years and find it works wonders. It can be used in the kitchen, bathroom and even on floors. It's naturally anti-bacterial, non-toxic, and much better than the chemical-laden versions that you can buy.

NATURAL MULTI-PURPOSE HOUSEHOLD CLEANER

INGREDIENTS
½ cup (4 fl oz/115 g) white vinegar
½ cup (4 fl oz/115 g) eucalyptus or tea tree oil
1 tsp baking soda
1 tsp natural, eco-friendly dishwashing liquid (available from supermarkets)
2 cups (8 fl oz/230 g) water
A few drops of lavender or orange essential oil can be added for fragrance (optional)
...

DIRECTION
Mix all the ingredients together in a spray bottle. Apply with a soft, clean cloth.

Chapter 5

ROOMS, THEIR FUNCTIONS AND BASIC LAYOUTS

*I like lots of air, order, personal objects
and beautiful architecture.*

William Hodgins, esteemed American interior designer

Entry Point

Dressing the front entrance of a home is one of my favorite areas to work on as it says so much about the occupant and sets the tone for the rest of the residence. First impressions last, so it's worthwhile giving weight to your home's entrance in your overall design. Interestingly, it is often neglected by home renovators as other interior rooms are given precedence, but I think it should be considered first.

Your home's entrance should be **polished** and **inviting**. Externally, lighting (for both security and to create a welcoming ambiance), house number, plants, and a doormat that are attractive and practical are important elements to include. The garden shouldn't be overlooked if it is positioned in front of your entry point.

Whether a small urban garden, or a sprawling country property, often this is a great source of enjoyment for both you and your guests so should be given adequate attention. The garden and path leading to your home can give your home street appeal so don't dress up your door, only to leave a rambling, neglected garden ruin the look that you want to achieve.

It might sound obvious, but an easily accessible entrance with a **well-defined path to the doorway** is essential. Many homes have entry points at the side, or around the back of the house, which are confusing and do not make for an attractive streetscape. If it isn't possible to move your front door, use a path and eye-catching pots of plants to draw visitors to your door.

With smart metal and glass options available, house numbers can make a decorative statement, and should be bold and clear at the front of the house.

If your house can accommodate them, **double front doors** look impressive and lend an air of grandeur. I like front doors to be glossy and ornate, while not being fussy or over elaborate. For this reason, timber doors with decorative molded panels are a good option. A couple of formal potted topiary trees can work wonders and provide instant appeal for visitors.

Entry points look best when they are **balanced** and **symmetrical**, so try to create this harmony at your front door. Unless your home is very modern, decorative details, such as shutters and awnings over windows, can provide additional detail. A climbing plant that has been shaped over or around a front entrance adds a lovely touch.

Colored doors are a bold statement, and when paired with a neutral surrounding palette can be visually very striking. Colored doorways are a great way to make your home stand out, show your personality, warm the space and bring it to life. In Feng Shui, the popular Chinese principle of design based on energy and balance, it is believed that a red front door is especially auspicious. It doesn't have to match, but it can be fun to paint both the exterior as well as the interior of a door in the same shade for continuity, and to brighten up the interior space.

Many larger homes have an **entry vestibule** or hallway. There is something quite distinguished and old fashioned about an entry hall. Far from wasted space, this area should be a luxurious and dramatic entry antechamber that gives a taste of what is to come inside the house. A hall table with a pretty display – perhaps a lamp, some fresh flowers and meaningful, stylish ornaments – looks chic and inviting. Depending on the shape of your hall, round tables can look supremely stylish, perhaps with an over-sized display of flowers, leaves or branches as a feature.

The hallway is also a space where you will often need to store coats, hats, bags, shoes and keys. Stylish hooks, a storage cupboard, or a coat and shoe rack will be a practical addition in this area of the home. Whatever you choose, make sure that it is an attractive storage option as the hallway gives visitors their first impression of your abode.

A mirror works well in a hallway too, as it allows you to check your appearance quickly prior to departing your home. You could place a mirror above an attractive chest of drawers sitting beside a coat rack – providing storage for your shoes within the drawers, coats and hats on the rack, and keys in a smart bowl on the top.

A statement light, either a chic hanging pendant, or an oversized table lamp can also make an entrance area spectacular. If you go out in the evening and leave the lamp on a timer, you'll be able to see clearly when you come home later.

In older homes, long, adding a skylight or a glass-paneled front door can enhance a dark passageway. Place an attractive painting, or small table with a decorative display at the end of the hallway to attract the eye there. Large horizontal striped paint or wallpaper on walls will also draw your eye down the space and give the illusion of a larger area.

On a practical level, the entry point often requires **storage** for one's shoes, coats, keys and other paraphernalia so make sure that however you store these items that the storage is chic! A smart silver 'key' box, or a table with drawers to conceal items is perfect. Stylish hooks for coats and hats, and a basket or chest for shoes are good options.

Kitchen

The kitchen is the beating heart of every home, the central meeting place where you nourish your body and feed your soul.

Kitchens were once designed with utility in mind. They were small, pokey and tucked away. Nowadays they are designed as an integral part of most modern homes and are usually in a prominent position close to, or part of, the living area. These days, kitchens are designed as a space to be used by all the family as well as for the traditional purpose of cooking and eating dinner. Kitchens are also expanding in size.

Kitchen design is a specialized area so it's worthwhile spending time researching the type of kitchen you want, working out how much storage you need and the gadgets that you require. Kitchen showrooms are fantastic for this as they give you so many options and ideas in one space.

Kitchens bring families together, and the design of your kitchen will determine whether this is true for you or not. I once lived in a home that had a small, awkward and dark kitchen that was at the back of the property, away from the living area. I hated cooking in that house. My new home has an open plan kitchen with a dining and sitting area in the one space, and spending time preparing food there is a joy. This is why design is so important – it can be the difference between a home that is a pleasure to spend time in, and one that is depressing and uninspiring.

An entirely new kitchen is a large investment so make sure you get it right the first time. The aim is to plan your kitchen design with at least a 20-year lifespan. The main design principle to follow when designing a kitchen is the 'work triangle'. This is the space between the three main points in the kitchen – the sink, the oven and the refrigerator. To maintain easy flow in the kitchen, the ideal distance between each is 4 ft/1200 mm, but up to 9 feet/2700 mm is acceptable. As with any rule, there are exceptions. If you have a kitchen that runs along a single wall then you will not be able to accommodate the three-point triangle, and in this situation you would consider the distance between the three elements in a straight line to create maximum ease of use.

If your kitchen has a suitably placed window, it is best to position the sink beneath it to allow light through and to give a pleasant vista from the workspace. The reflection from the sink will also add light to the room.

The most impressive kitchens don't have visible electrical equipment, freestanding bins, or clutter on work surfaces and they have **concealed white goods** – refrigerator and dishwasher, plus microwave and other electrical equipment such as toasters and kettles. An **integral oven** and **large pantry storage area** are also crucial in a new kitchen, as is rubbish/garbage disposal. These built in and concealed items should have a front panel in the same finish as the rest of the kitchen and should be flush with the cabinet doors to create a continuous look, unbroken to the eye. Overhead cabinets should reach the ceiling or run flush with a bulkhead. In the same vein, very modern kitchens will rarely have handles on cabinets, instead opting for invisible angled finger-pull cupboards and drawers, or push-pull ones.

In very large kitchens, a separate preparation area with smaller sink and bench space, plus baking areas for rolling dough or other culinary delights might be included. In these larger kitchens, the triangular 'zones' may start to overlap and create secondary three-way relationships between important areas.

Island benches have also become popular again. They add valuable extra bench and storage space. The added benefit is that they can also double as a dining space if they have an overhang and bench seating on one side. In terms of lighting – it is very fashionable to hang a series of pendant lights over island benches. Three pendants over an island bench look very chic, hung so that visibility is maintained across the kitchen while either standing or sitting. Think about installing a sink or stovetop in the island if you are low on bench space elsewhere in the kitchen. This will also allow you to face your guests or children while preparing meals.

Lighting can be concealed within glass cabinets to show off glassware and china, or recessed underneath overhead cabinets to shed light on to the bench or stovetop below.

Rangehoods with extractor fans also often include lighting that illuminates the space below in one multi-functional product.

Splashbacks are an important decorative element and can dramatically affect the look of a kitchen. In recent times they have become the design focus of the modern kitchen as there are so many artful options available. They are also relatively easy to update by removing the existing tiles or material in use, and placing the new splashback in its place without having to remove everything around it. The most popular materials used for splashbacks are tiles, glass, stainless steel, and acrylic surfaces. Whatever you choose, the main concern is that the splashback is going to be waterproof and easy to clean.

Tiles are a popular choice for splashbacks and there are so many choices available in size, shape, color and pattern so you can really individualize your kitchen. Be aware that small tiles such as mosaics will create more work as the grout will require regular cleaning. Large sheets of custom cut glass are popular and practical as they just require a quick wipe down to clean them. You can even have LED lights fitted behind some glass splashbacks to throw light into your kitchen. Selecting the right color is so important as garish colors will date quickly. Some timeless options are made in classic colors such as beige, white, or a soft natural green blue (the color of glass).

Similarly, sheets of custom fit stainless steel look modern and industrial, and will be easy to clean. For a more old world look you can use pressed tin panels, which are embedded with a pattern of your choice. These were popular on ceilings in the early 1900s and were often painted. They are a versatile product and can be used in kitchens, bathrooms, on ceilings and as wall features.

If you want a seamless look, you can continue your benchtop material as a splashback. Obviously the splashback section will either be a thin laminate or it will be a stone veneer and not as thick as your benchtop.

Benchtops should be thick and robust, with no obvious joins if using a laminate or veneer. The best (and usually the most expensive) choices are stone such as granite and marble, or a stone composite, that give a luxurious look and will last for years. To minimize cost on natural stone, you could elect to have a deep edging on a thin slab. You can choose how you would like the edge of your bench top to look too – popular choices include square, which gives a modern effect, or bullnose, which is rounded. You can also elect to have a more elaborate edge with scallops and fine sculpting.

Before

After

Essentially a paint, 2-pack polyurethane – often referred to as a 2-pack – is a popular choice for benchtops and cupboards in very modern, streamlined kitchens. It comes in a high gloss finish and is durable and long lasting.

Timber benchtops are beautiful in the right type of kitchen – a country or rustic style for example. However, timber can warp and scratch over time. Also, it needs to be oiled regularly. Polished concrete is an affordable, modern option and looks great in contemporary, industrial-style kitchens.

Double power points should be installed at various places in the kitchen as most modern appliances require a power source. Don't scrimp on basic fittings as the detail makes the impact.

Update a tired kitchen without completing an entirely new renovation by focusing on details such as the benchtop, splashback, handles and stovetop. Replace only the doors of cabinets, rather than the entire cabinet itself. Or, if they're in acceptable condition, the cupboard doors and benchtop can be sprayed using a new technology called resurfacing. Many homeowners use this service when they are selling as it provides an instant result for minimum outlay. Where once the paint would chip off within months, the results are now extraordinary and will last for several years. Avoid DIY tile paints, however, as these chip and are obvious to the eye on close inspection.

Flat-pack kitchens can be ordered online. In fact, I know several home decorators who have ordered entire flat pack kitchens from abroad, then sourced and added details such as benchtops and splashbacks themselves. You will need accurate measurements and a good carpenter to install the kitchen for you, unless you are very handy and have experience with such things. As with any purchase online, you should also be wary of inferior quality products as these can be a false economy.

If you want a shiny new kitchen without having to go to the expense of a custom designed one from a fancy kitchen supplier, you can use cabinets and shelving from a *reliable* global supplier such as IKEA, then add trimmings to give the kitchen flair. Paint cabinets a custom color, add decorative moldings, stylish handles such as white china knobs or shiny steel grips, and a stone worktop to disguise its origins, if you like.

Ample storage is essential in a properly functioning kitchen – with modern convenience comes an array of household goods that require space. If these things clutter your bench space it can affect the enjoyment of your kitchen. Likewise adequate pantry space according to your needs is vital. If your kitchen is small, consider building into wall cavities for extra space.

If you are using existing space in your kitchen for your pantry, you can use clever storage helpers to maximize the space you have available. Say you have an overhead cupboard that has one shelf in it. You can purchase 'steps' that sit inside the cupboard that will give you additional space for cans and bottles, and also help you find items that might get lost at the back of the space. Another option for making cupboards more accessible is to buy a round lazy Susan that will rotate allowing you to spin your pantry items around without having to reach to the back and knock over all the items in front. Lazy Susans come in a range of sizes.

Pull-out pantries are fantastic for smaller kitchens as they allow access to items from both sides. They are set on runners that pull out into the kitchen so that you don't have to get lost inside a dark, shallow space each time you are looking for something.

Flooring options include laminate, vinyl, tiles, or timber. It's important to remember that there will inevitably be spills and splashes in a kitchen so the flooring that's easiest to clean is going to be best.

If your kitchen is used for entertaining regularly, and is the hub of social activity in your home, introduce some glamorous items such as hanging pendant lamps, a rug, and furniture that can be moved in and out as and when the occasion requires.

Dining and entertaining

The perfect dining room should be able to host an intimate dinner for two or a party of 20.

The dining table is the focal point of the room, so should be striking in design and be surrounded by comfortable chairs. Tables that extend are brilliant as they allow room for when extra guests arrive.

If your room will accommodate it, a sideboard to house crockery, cutlery and glassware is not only practical but also an attractive feature in a dining space. If you only have a small area, a compact but stylish drinks trolley or bar cart will give your room some glamour and make serving drinks a breeze.

A statement light above the dining table can create the right mood for dining and be a talking point for guests. It doesn't have to be a single light; you could hang two or three pendant lights from the ceiling at varying heights for a dramatic style statement. Ensure that the lights are high enough that there is a clear line of sight across the table when seated.

On one of the walls surrounding your dining table there should be an attractive artwork to make the view from the table more appealing.

When your table is not in use, dress it with a stylish bowl as a centerpiece; a large vase of flowers, or two glass lanterns with candles so that it doesn't look bare.

Entertaining guests at home became a lost art for some time as the fast pace of modern life meant that social events and celebrations were held at restaurants. Now we are seeing a return to the enjoyment of hosting guests in one's home.

As a child my family loved to hold lavish lunch, brunch and dinner parties at home. Abundant with food, flowers and friends, these events always created special memories of good times. Getting dressed up and styling the house were always a big part of the festivities.

If you are entertaining at home, your guests will appreciate personal touches such as hand-written place cards on the table, fresh flowers, candles and stylish hand towels in the bathroom.

To create a beautiful table, decorations don't have to be expensive or elaborate, and in fact, many of the most beautiful table settings I've seen have used props from nature or household items.

I recently saw a stunning table setting with butcher's paper as a table runner, big glass bowls of lemons as centerpieces, lots of tea lights, and cut crystal glassware, all atop a distressed timber table. The results were understated yet so stylish. The butcher's paper was a genius addition as the host had written each guest's name in front of their place in pretty scroll writing with a thick marker. The combination of the textures in the paper and glass added the detail and interest rather than a busy over-styled table.

If your handwriting is not up to scratch then print pretty sticky labels from your computer, place them on place cards, and add some ribbon through a small hole punched in the top.

Be a gracious host and introduce any invitees who may not know each other.

Living Room

If the kitchen is the heart of the home, then the living area is the blood coursing through its veins. It is usually the most **social** area of the home and should be designed with lifestyle and comfort in mind.

A living room should be comfortable, stylish and expressive of your character. Most often, it is a place for lounging and relaxing. Many new homes have open-plan kitchens, dining and lounge areas so you should consider how the space will be used before selecting furniture and décor.

Whether you live alone, or have a large family, the living room is where most of your time will be spent, and as such, should be given appropriate weight when designing your home.

Built in cabinetry is ideal in a living area to conceal television and entertainment units for those times when you are entertaining in a more formal fashion. There are companies who specialize in this, and many carpenters will also design built-in cupboard space for you. Think about how much of the cabinet you want open to display decorative personal items such as photographs, books and ornaments, and how much you want to be able to hide away.

Select **furniture** for a living room according to how you are going to use the space. There are many styles of seating available so to be sure that you select the correct size and shape you should start by drawing a plan of the room.

Modular or sectional sofas often work well for the modern home as they are easily interchangeable according to your needs. L-shapes are popular, providing a convenient place to put your feet up, as are sofa beds that can provide extra sleeping space for visitors. A more formal look is usually achieved with a living room suite – a sofa with two matching armchairs

Most couches are upholstered, and the **choice of upholstery** can make a huge difference to the look and longevity of your couch. Avoid the lure of cheap fabrics as they will be a false economy. Faux suede is now out of vogue but other types of fabric such as linen are a mainstay of couch upholstery due to their practicality.

Soft leather is a good option as it is classic, practical and stylish, especially if of a good quality and slightly distressed finish. Think Ralph Lauren.

Most upholstery fabrics have ratings according to their durability, so it's worth choosing one that has a high rating to see you through years of wear. Commercial grade fabrics are generally very practical as they undergo extensive testing to ensure that they will last in high traffic venues.

If your upholstery has seen better days, you can have your seating re-upholstered by a professional for a small percentage of what it would cost to buy a new sofa. However, it's worth researching to find out whether it's going be more economical to re-upholster or buy new. Mass-produced furniture is now cheaper than ever before so obtain a few quotes for re-upholstering. It may be that by the time you've bought fabric and paid the upholsterer, it may be more costly than you anticipated. If your sofa is merely stained and not permanently soiled, steam cleaning is a great way to give it a new lease of life. It's also wise to spray your sofa once a year with a protective spray that will act as a barrier to future marks.

Custom-made slip covers are a great way to protect your sofa if your seating has a lot of use – young children and teenagers, for example. Many companies make these and will include stylish designer details such as piping in a contrasting color, and a modern skirt around the base of your sofa, which lends a finishing touch.

Ready-made slip covers might be a more affordable option, but are not as good as custom made, and may look untidy and ill fitting.

The **shape of the couch** is a very important consideration as well as its style helping to create the look and feel of the room. Modern and square sofas looks great in a contemporary home. A rounded shape with diamond tufting is a more classic option.

When ordering a new couch, you should consider the **materials used in the construction of the framework** as well as the inner springs and cushion inserts, as the

quality can vary dramatically. The traditional material used in the past was hardwood, but aluminum, plastic and laminated boards are now more common.

Hard, synthetic foam pad inserts can be quite uncomfortable, so either a combination of feather, down and foam, or feather and down combined, is best. If, after time, your sofa starts to slump and won't hold its shape, you can have your seat cushion inserts 'wrapped' in new foam to extend their life span.

A coffee table is the focal point in a living room. When choosing the style you should consider size, shape and use before purchasing. Do you have small children that are likely to be running around your living room? If so, a glass table isn't going to be your best option. If you have lots of books or a need for storage, then you might want to select a table that can accommodate these beneath, either in chic baskets, or in drawers.

Styling your coffee table has become something of an art in recent times. The fun part about this is that it can be ever evolving according to your tastes and mood. An obvious choice is a stack or two of stylish books, a candle in an attractive canister, a small bonsai plant or flowers, and whatever else it is that might take your fancy. Don't overcrowd your table, and again, use the rules of balance and harmony to create an aesthetically pleasing display.

You don't have to stick to one coffee table either, if you have a large room, often matching tables placed side-by-side look sophisticated. Conventional coffee tables are not your only option – a stylish silver, gold or timber tray atop an upholstered ottoman is a chic addition to any living area.

Bedroom

A bedroom is a place for rest and rejuvenation, a personal sanctuary in which to recharge at the end of each day. As such, the décor should be serene, inviting and void of clutter.

The **best color palettes** for bedrooms are usually muted and calming. Soft colors such as pale blue, green and cream are good choices, as are soft mauve and beige. If you like a little more punch you can use navy blue and caramel, or a deeper shade of a pastel as an accent. Introduce two hues and their tonal values when you add textured or solid and patterned fabrics and you will create a room that is serene. Strong colors in any room setting tend to incite anger and anxiety.

Storage for personal items, clothing and shoes should be central to the design of your bedroom. Freestanding bedroom furniture can be very attractive, but for maximum use of the space, built in is best.

Soft flooring such as carpet is a luxurious addition to a bedroom, but if you prefer hard flooring such as timber floorboards, then a large rug can help soften the effect.

Designer tip: Matching side tables are considered best in Feng Shui for harmony and balance.

Lighting in a bedroom should be soft and tranquil, so use soft glow, low wattage globes, and use side lamps at night to calm your senses. Dimmer switchers are ideal in a bedroom so that you can adjust the amount of light according to need.

Bedroom furniture such as beds should be comfortable, and nightstands or bedside tables should be practical. Upholstered bedheads are fashionable and also practical as they are comfortable to rest your back against while sitting in bed.

Nightstands should have adequate space for lighting, as well as storage for items such as books, photographs, an alarm clock and any other items that you like to keep beside the bed. They should also be the correct height for your bed, and should match. Mis-matched side tables can work in some rooms – bohemian or eclectic style bedrooms, for example – but for the most upmarket and professional look, choose matching side tables.

Artwork in a bedroom should be subtle. If you have a statement piece, make it into a feature above a bed. Art is a very subjective choice, but charcoal illustrations of the human body, botanical illustrations or painterly, soft abstract artworks are my preferred option due to their soothing nature.

Who said nights were for sleep?
...
Marilyn Monroe

Parents' retreats are increasing in popularity as mums and dads look for their own space in homes crowded with children and their friends. Often larger than traditionally sized bedrooms, they can accommodate a Queen or King size bed and include an additional sitting area with sofa or comfortable armchairs for space to relax and take some time out.

If you want to introduce a sitting area into your standard sized bedroom, you can create bench seating under a window. A mass of comfortable cushions with storage beneath will complete this practical and cozy seating option. If your room won't accommodate this feature, a freestanding upholstered bench seat at the end of the bed, or a snug, welcoming armchair in the corner of the room may provide seating.

Comfort is key here as the bedroom should be a haven away from the hustle and bustle of the rest of the home. Many parents' retreats will also include a large walk-in wardrobe to house clothing and accessories, a double bathroom, and a balcony or courtyard with an outdoor setting that offers a peaceful space to unwind outside. If you must have a television in the bedroom, conceal it within a cabinet, or have one installed that automatically rises from within an attractive piece of furniture such as a chest or trunk positioned at the end of the bed.

Dressing rooms and wardrobes for storage of clothing, shoes and accessories shouldn't be considered less important than the rest of the space, and should be just as aesthetically pleasing.

In both the smallest and grandest of wardrobes, order and structure are most important to organize your possessions and make it easy to find the items you need each day. Why not display your most attractive accessories such as hats, handbags and jewelry? Open shelving can work well for this. You can either organize your things by color, or by item, for example, putting all of your trousers together, all of your dresses together, and so on.

With shoes, I think it best to display those in collections of styles – sandals, pumps, boots and so on. Stuff the toes of your shoes to keep them in perfect condition, and place supports in the legs of tall boots to stand them upright to keep their shape. Create a 'shoe library' with clear boxes to make it easy to identify shoes so that you have everyday items on hand. Alternatively, wall mounted, extendable or tiered racks are perfect for storing multiple pairs of shoes neatly in a smaller area. Matching hangers help the space look uniform and neat.

Externally, decorative moldings added to the outside of your wardrobe can add a grand appearance to a basic piece. For smaller bedrooms, mirrored doors can add the illusion of more space.

Beds that are set up against a built-in display unit are gaining in popularity and you can use the wall space around the bed to house books and ornaments, as well as build in a custom-made bedside table or two. Consider lining the back of the open shelving with pretty wallpaper for a designer edge.

When choosing a bed, invest for the long term. We spend an average eight hours sleeping per night, which equates to 25 years of sleep by the time you are 75 – roughly one third of your life. When you think about it like that, the importance of good bedding is immediately apparent. If you can't invest in a new bed as part of your new look, consider buying a 'mattress topper' that fits over the top of the mattress and sits under your mattress protector or bottom sheet. They are usually feather or foam filled and add an extra layer of comfort to sleep on.

Bed linen should be good quality. High thread count, natural fiber linens are now available for a fraction of the price they used to be, so it's worthwhile having a couple of interchangeable sets. Synthetic sheets are an inferior choice as they can be hot and uncomfortable as your body temperature fluctuates during the night and, after a short time, will usually start to pill making them uncomfortable to sleep on.

For a calm, stylish bedroom you can't beat crisp, white bed linen. There is nothing like getting into a freshly made bed at the end of a long day. Think how good it feels getting into bed at a luxury hotel – why shouldn't you have that kind of luxury at home? Strongly patterned or brightly colored sheets or covers should be reserved for accessories (which you can change by the seasons) or for children's rooms to make it more appealing for them to go to bed each night.

Large European pillows placed as highlights on your bed look luxurious, as do shams (cylindrical cushions). **A bedskirt** or valance is the finishing touch, hiding the lower mattress or bedframe and giving you a streamlined look in the room.

Ventilation and lighting are important in bedrooms too. Make sure you have adequate window openings to the outdoors and install enough lighting to make the room glow without being bright.

DIY headboards are gaining regard as home decorators look for ways to add personality to their bedrooms. Some options include painting a vintage timber headboard in a fun, new color, for example, covering an old headboard in a slip cover that sits loosely over the top. Personalize this with an initial monogram and you have instant 'wow' factor. Upholstered bedheads are the height of chic and are relatively easy to create at home – you'll need a piece of board, some foam, upholstery tacks, glue, and your chosen fabric. Consider making your headboard twice the usual height of a bedhead to add stature to a small room. You can hang two ready-made canvases covered in a favorite fabric above a bed to act as a frame for the bed without the expense of a substantial bedhead.

Upholstered walls add elegance and panache to a space. Most often the walls will have to be prepared, lined and padded to give the upholstery the right finished look,

so there is a cost to be borne in mind, if this is what you desire. There is a reason that this walling is not uncommon in palaces and other regal homes around the world – they want a certain look and have the budget to match. Silks and velvets are good choices for upholstered walls as they are plush, luxurious and sophisticated.

When it comes to decorating with **accessories** in your bedroom, remember that less is best. Clutter does nothing for serenity and is not good for the psyche.

Baby Boy Nursery

Children's bedrooms need to be multi-functional to accommodate the various needs of the child. Decoration should have a sense of fun as well as being practical. From the time a new-born baby comes home, making the bedroom functional for the age group is important. Choosing the right shelving means that it can be adapted for the different iterations of a child's room. When buying a bed, consider one that has storage beneath or one that can store a trundle bed below for sleepovers.

Stylish window treatments also help to make a child's room look cultivated. A striped pelmet with a plain curtain will give a kid's room a finished and professional look. If you don't have a pelmet, and your budget won't stretch to one, add in a detail such as some tassel tie backs, which will give a similar effect (just be careful with toddlers as they can get caught in them and turn into a strangling hazard). Similarly don't hang anything heavy, including picture frames, over a cot or child's bed as they can fall on them and cause considerable damage. Secure any heavy furniture to the wall in small children's rooms too, to avoid them pulling bookshelves or a chest of drawers down onto themselves.

The chicest children's rooms are those that strike a balance between being childlike and stylish. Create a chic kid's space that doesn't lose its style by adding one or two funky details, such as a striking light, and use a color palette that is fun but stylish – instead of baby blue, or baby pink, choose a tone that has more depth but is still bright.

Accessories for kid's rooms are fun, and don't have to be expensive if you're inventive. You can make bunting from old fabric and twine, a mural wall painted by the whole family, or a mobile with paper origami. Some children love to be up high, so create layers with multi-functional furniture. Consider a bunk bed with a desk beneath.

Don't forget essentials such as desk and wardrobe. Storage is important as children have so many toys and books to hide away. Ultimately, a child's room should be a **space for learning and creativity** to thrive through play and imagination.

A'bell child pinpoint her ambrophobia
to the day she discovered her favourite jumper
had shrunk after being washed

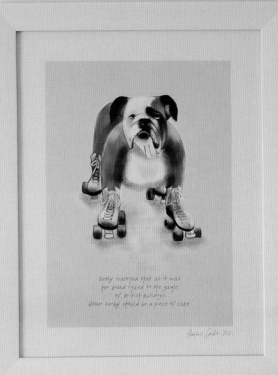

Betty reasoned that as it was
her breed linked to the game
of British bulldog,
roller derby should be a piece of cake

Every now and then, when Farmer Troy was out,
Ray snuck up to the farm shed
and borrowed the quad bike

Gavin hated being such a self conscious walker
the more he thought about it,
the more it looked as though he was attempting
a forward moonwalk on jelly.

Bathroom

Bathrooms often get overlooked in the style department, with stark whites and neutrals being the easy go-to color palette in a wet area. I love a crisp, white bathroom, but if you want to make a statement, you can **amplify yours with exaggerated decorative features** such as wallpaper, decorative tiles, mirrors, lighting and surface materials.

In terms of bathroom design, issues of space in small bathrooms can be overcome with some clever design tricks. Small bathrooms look great with feature wallpaper in a wide horizontal stripe to give the illusion of more space and distract from the fact that you're in a small room. Wallpaper is not just for walls, you could keep your walls clean and consider wallpaper on the ceiling of your bathroom with a striking light for instant wow factor.

If you are re-designing your bathroom, or starting from scratch, it's important that the toilet is not the first thing that you see as you enter. A toilet does not make for a style statement! Similarly you should carefully consider the scale and placement of all elements including towel rails and toilet paper holders. Seemingly minor details are essential to get correct in the design as they are used so frequently, and can become a source of serious frustration if not placed at the correct height or in the right position in the scheme of things.

Dramatize your space with one major statement piece – for example, a beautiful vanity, or a freestanding bath.

Don't be afraid to mix old with new. The juxtaposition of aged and new items can look fabulous. A freshly tiled bathroom with modern tiles, set against a vintage mirror and towel holder can look tremendously chic.

Reflective surfaces work very well in bathrooms. An entire wall of mirrored tiles looks gorgeous in the right space.

If your bathroom is dated, you can employ the same tricks in that room as in the kitchen – namely **resurfacing**. Enamel baths and basins can be resurfaced, giving them the appearance of new items, as can cabinets and benchtops. Some new tiles and a new mirror or two will complete this makeover.

I like **house plants** in bathrooms, but because of the steam and low light levels, it's important to choose the right ones or keeping the plant alive will be a challenge. Heart-leaf philodendrons, maidenhair ferns and spider plants can withstand the humid conditions in the bathroom with some care. Peace lilies (also called Madonna lilies) and bromeliads are also hardy options.

Black toilets, vanities, tiles and decorative accessories such as marble toothbrush holders are coming to prominence and lend an air of glamour. Just be selective with your black items, don't overcrowd the room with black accessories or you will run the

risk of making the room too dark. One or two accents work well. Alternatively, a black tiled wall with a lighter color for fittings and fixtures such as toilets and vanity units work well.

Home Office and Spare Room

With the way we live today, many homes **need to be multi-functional,** especially in small homes, or those in which lots of people live.

Home office
Home offices are popular as it's now easier to work remotely with technological advances and the growth of the Internet and electronic mail. The trick is **integrating your office space into your home** so that you end up with a functional, inspiring space where you can be productive.

If you are decorating a home office, it needs to be streamlined, orderly and functional first. Then you can add in the detail.

Purpose-made office furniture is often not the most inspiring to purchase. Out of the ordinary items in a home office can work very well. A striking hanging pendant light over the desk, chic window coverings, and a statement rug can all make the space a place you want to go to each morning. You can also introduce **interesting wall art** with inspiring quotes and beautiful images.

In order to create a space in which to **focus and be productive,** it's important to locate the office away from the main living areas of the home, if possible, otherwise there will be many distractions.

It's important to have **adequate lighting** in a work space. Make the most of natural light if you can. Alternatively, bright lights from overhead lighting and desk lamps will provide adequate lighting in your office.

Spare Room

The spare room provides a brilliant opportunity to design a multi-use space. By being creative with layout and furniture selection, you can create a guest bedroom come study; or a children's play room that converts into a reading room or sun room for adults when the toys and games are packed away. If a room doesn't have a purpose, it can all too easily become a dumping ground to hide junk when visitors pop in. Whether it be a basement, attic, shed or just an additional room in your home that's not being used, if designed correctly you can make the most of this space.

The key to creating a successful multi-use space is about how functional your furniture and storage is. Look for ready-made multi-purpose furniture, or design your own and have a carpenter make it for you. Pinterest is a great source of images for inspiration for something like this. Just type what you're looking for 'multi-purpose kids furniture' for example, and you will find many pictures to set you on the road to a beautiful result.

In a children's playroom, you could create a reading nook for adults in the corner of the room for use when the kids are asleep or away from the house. Built-in bench seating with storage beneath and lots of comfortable cushions would make this attractive for both uses. In a situation such as this, attractive storage is vital, so built-in cupboards, toy boxes with lids and closed shelving will allow you to feel as if you're in your own space, and not just sitting in the kid's play area.

If you have open bookshelves, use smart looking storage boxes or baskets to place games and toys inside so that they are not on display. From a decorative point of view, you don't have to use kid's fabrics with childlike motifs, but rather brighten the space and keep everyone happy with fabrics and colors that appeal to both young and old. A good example of this would be *toile de jouy*. Available in very pretty designs, toile is a type of cloth fabric that originated in France and tells a 'story' by depicting a scene of people in a repeated pattern over a white background. It is youthful whilst still being sophisticated so ideal for this type of application.

DO WHAT YOU LOVE EVERY DAY

GO CONFIDENTLY IN THE DIRECTION OF YOUR DREAMS LIVE THE LIFE YOU'VE IMAGINED

(THOREAU)

Chapter 6

MAXIMIZE YOUR SPACE

One can furnish a room very luxuriously
by taking out furniture rather than
putting it in.

The late Francis Jourdain, French furniture maker

Visual tricks to open up your home

A small space doesn't have to mean a less impressive one – making a small area seem larger is all about tricking the eye to create the illusion of a larger area. Infuse your interiors with light and energy and your compact space will instantly feel generous.

Use the same color on walls and ceilings. Paint the walls, ceiling, beams, architrave, doors and any ceiling details such as architectural moldings in the same color to open the ceiling space. By doing this, you will restrict distracting details so that the eye reads a solid color.

Hang artworks low. Another trick is to hang artwork lower on the wall to exaggerate the upper wall area and ceiling height.

Use neutral colors. It's no secret that light, neutral colors help to visually open up a room. The key is a monochromatic scheme. You don't have to stick to white – lighter tones of beige and gray will do the same trick bouncing light around the room.

It's wise to steer away from bright feature walls - go for one consistent color throughout the area but add interest by introducing accessories and furnishings in different shades and textures of the neutral color.

Adjoining rooms should also be painted in the same or similar shades to create the feeling of spaciousness.

It's a good idea to match furniture to your wall color. By doing this, your furniture will recede and make the room feel larger.

Reflective surfaces such as high gloss and shiny surfaces reflect light so a few metallic finishes on furniture and accessories help bring light into a small space.

Mirrors are also very effective tools when trying to create the illusion of a larger environment. Don't forget that mirrors will reflect whatever is opposite, so be sure to

hang the mirror facing something attractive. Multiples of mirrors also look good so consider hanging a series of two or three on your wall to make a stylish statement.

Create areas or 'zones' within an open plan space. Many small homes have an open living, dining, kitchen space. Divide this space into areas for specific use through careful placement of furniture. A room full of furniture without any specific zones will be overwhelming on the eye and therefore appear overcrowded.

Screens are great for visually dividing a room, as are area rugs, as well as distinctive furniture for each 'space' within the space.

Clever Storage ideas can use every nook and cranny effectively - awkward corners and unused space under stairways can be transformed into clever storage units. It's best to have storage built in, but if your budget won't allow this, look for modular storage units that can be adjusted to fit various sizes of space.

Dramatic details can make a small room appear instantly grand by adding a feature; a decorative accessory such as a chandelier. Just be careful with proportion. You don't want to dominate the room with something that is oversized and out of scale with the rest of the room, especially if you have low ceilings.

Low furniture works well in small spaces. Avoid tall furniture as it will interrupt the eye line around the room and make the space seem smaller. The use of horizontal lines will help to create a seemingly larger space. Think low and not tall for furniture to create an uninterrupted eye's view across the room.

Contrary to popular belief, however, a small space doesn't mean you need to use only small furniture. Without overcrowding the room, **one large feature piece of furniture** among smaller items can look fabulous. For example, you could add a statement armchair in the corner of the lounge room, among smaller pieces. Use an interesting fabric – a textured fabric such as velvet or textured linen will add punch to the room without cluttering it.

Clear furniture made from Perspex or glass is perfect in a small space as you can see through it, giving the illusion of more room. Popular during the 1970s, this type of furniture is making a strong and stylish comeback.

Furniture that has space **underneath** it will make a room seem larger: a small console table is perfect in a small room.

The position of furniture in a small room is important. It's often assumed that a space will seem larger if all the furniture is pushed against the wall, but this is not the case. **By bringing furniture in from the walls,** you create volume around it, resulting in the appearance of a visually larger space. Furniture pulled just a few inches in from the walls can create a big difference.

Custom-built storage is perfect in a small space. Use all the space available – a custom-built floor-to-ceiling bookshelf can house books, ornaments, a television and entertainment system, artworks, even a pull-out desk. Also consider unused space under stairways to add custom-built features.

Multi-functional furniture such as bench seating is a perfect example of furniture that can serve a multitude of uses. It can store goods within it, act as seating if a table is positioned up against it, or as stand alone seating in a lounge area. Nesting tables are a great multi-functional item too – the smaller tables underneath can be used in a variety of ways when needed.

As you can see, with some clever styling, you can create the feeling of a space in a small area.

Lighting for maximum impact

Lighting is one of the most important elements in a home. Some consider it the magic ingredient in design. It can create drama, airiness, a solemn atmosphere or a bright, fun one. The quality of light in your home is integral to your wellbeing.

The importance of lighting cannot be undervalued. However gorgeous the room and furniture, if the lighting is dull, the room won't shine as it should. Illuminate your rooms, and your home will be an alluring place to spend time.

If you are renovating or building a new home, it's worth speaking to a lighting specialist to get the best result. They will take into consideration how you use each room, how much natural light the space receives, and provide you with a solution that complements the way that you live in the space. They can also save you money in the long run with the installation of energy-saving solutions such as modern low voltage or LED lights.

Modern recessed ceiling lighting can create unflattering shadows and has gone out of vogue. The new fashion is for a more elaborate style of lighting. Oversized table lamps, stylish pendant lights suspended from the ceiling, and wall sconces are more striking. Always choose warm toned bulbs, and in lamps, low wattage is best. Harsh and flat lighting will make living areas seem cold and uninviting.

The general rule of thumb is that there should be light sources at various levels or heights in the room, plus task lighting for specific needs if necessary. Dimmers are a good idea as they allow you to adjust the level of light in the room for varying conditions and requirements. It can be more soothing in the evening to sit in a soft light, rather than a bright one, for example. Dimmers can be placed on most light sources, including overhead lighting and lamps. Another benefit is that dimmers lengthen the life of a bulb and make the light more energy efficient.

Over a dining table, there should be a bold light to draw people in, and highlight the table beneath. For this reason, chandeliers, or other handing pendant lights are a good choice. Limit the wattage to 100 watts so that it's not too strong.

If you are highlighting the table, keep lighting in the rest of the room softer and more gentle. Wall sconces are a traditional form of lighting that provide a soft glow, and look stylish. They look best when matched and hung symmetrically at each side of a piece of furniture.

In the bathroom you will want overhead lighting as well as some sidelights for shaving and applying makeup.

In the kitchen, you will need overhead lighting and task lighting for cutting and preparing food. If you have overhead cabinets, you can install lighting beneath to illuminate the workspace below. It's also a good idea to light the stove from above. Often extractor fans above stoves will also include a light making them a multi-functional choice. Put different lights in different zones so you can adjust them accordingly and have a practical zone for cooking and a mood zone for entertaining.

In the bedroom, soft light that mimics candlelight is best. Bedside tables with attractive side lamps with low wattage bulbs are most suitable. If you have overhead lighting that is on a track or recessed and can be angled, face them away from the bed.

Types of lights
Flush mounted lights are installed directly into the ceiling, without any overhang. When you have enough, they will light up a whole room and give a modern appearance.

Semi-flush mounted lights hang lower than flush mounted, but not as low as a pendant light so allow for more head space underneath.

Pendant lights hang from the ceiling by a chain or cord. These are best used in rooms with taller ceiling heights. They come in a variety of fashionable styles to allow you to personalize your space and use them as a chic statement in a room.

Recessed lights are set into the ceiling and are usually able to be directed at a certain angle to highlight various objects or areas in the room. They give a modern, clean and streamlined look.

Track lighting contains bulbs that are placed along a track mounted to the ceiling. The benefit of track lighting is that you can adjust the light to face any angle and can often move the lights along the track as well, making it perfect to highlight artworks or other features in the room.

Lamps can either be a floor (standard) lamp, or a table lamp. They should be the right size so that when you are sitting in a chair or in bed reading, the shade is a little below your line of sight and you don't have a bright light in your eyes.

Wall sconces should also be placed so that the shades are also below your line of sight, once again avoiding a bright light in your eyes.

Pendant lights should not obstruct anyone's path through the room (that is, they shouldn't have to duck to avoid hitting them with their head). They also shouldn't obstruct the line of sight in the room.

Chandeliers, if hung over a table, should be at least one half to three quarters of the width of the table to cast the right amount of light and be the right proportion. Hang it so that it doesn't obstruct views across the table, but not so high that it's lost in the ceiling.

Lighting is everything.
It creates atmosphere, drama,
and intrigue in a room.

...

Martyn Lawrence Bullard,
British interior designer, author,
and television personality

Chapter 7

RESEARCH AND SOURCE

Nothing comes cheap, though the educated eye will always spot very nice things for the least money.

Albert Hadley, prominent late American interior designer

Where to source furniture, fabrics and soft furnishings

I love the challenge of creating a designer look for less, and if you know how to shop, you can **create luxury on a budget.** The best interiors are a combination of both cheap and cheerful, as well as some more expensive items in the mix.

Good quality furniture is where you should start when you design a room, then move from there to mix in more economical pieces. High-end furniture can be an expensive investment and should be part of your home for years to come. Many home decorators rush in and purchase expensive items without considering them in context of their home as a whole. For this reason, before embarking on a shopping expedition, it is best to **have a plan** – do a **stocktake** of your existing furniture, work out **what can be re-used** and then what you really need in terms of new items. If you have a 'wow' piece of furniture, use this as inspiration for the rest of your design.

If you don't want to pay full retail price, there are a few alternatives: wait until sale time, usually twice a year; purchase factory second items that might have slight imperfections; or purchase through a **discount online retailer** that specializes in designer homewares.

As with fashion retail, interior retail stores are heading online and offer considerable discounts. Many of these discount online stores will offer **membership** through a newsletter in which you will receive their latest offers. Their items extend from furniture to table and bed linens, china and artwork.

While a lot of high-end furniture and fabric suppliers will only deal with trade – meaning that you have to be an architect or designer to order from them – many **fabric houses** will have sales several times a year when they sell offcuts and end of rolls to the public. It's worth checking these sales as they may have just the amount you require to have a set of curtains or cushions made. A lot of fabric wholesalers are also moving online and offer fantastic designer patterns and looks so it's worthwhile searching on the Internet for a fabric that you love. Order a swatch before you purchase an entire quantity to check the quality and weight of the fabric as you'll need to ensure that it's suitable for the application that you will be using it for. A lightweight muslin won't be suitable for curtains, or furniture upholstery, for example.

Heritage building stores, reclamation yards and even **the local tip** can be great places to find **unique furniture items.** As they say, one man's trash is another man's treasure. Most areas will have a heritage building store that collects building items from properties that are being demolished or renovated. Expect to find rare and unique windows, doors, gates, garden statues and fireplaces. Mostly one-off, the exciting thing about sourcing like this is that no one else will have the same item or look as you, which is refreshing in an age when most things are mass produced.

If you go to the tip, you will need patience and determination as the items won't be restored, polished and displayed attractively. The upside is that you won't be paying inflated prices so it's a great place to find a true bargain.

Search and subscribe to the best lifestyle and interior blogs as they can be a brilliant source of information on sales and events where you can pick up a bargain, not to mention ideas and inspiration.

It's worth spending the time finding a blog that is run professionally as these will have the most current, up to date information - more than magazines, which are usually only published monthly.

In a minimal interior, what you don't do is as important as what you do.

...

Nate Berkus

Chapter 8

Use Color, Texture and Pattern Confidently

I owe my color sense to crayons.

Angelo Rafael Donghia, Acclaimed American interior designer

Angelo Rafael Donghia's quote about crayons is wonderful because too often people take the decorating of their homes too seriously.

Design is about expression and fun, and should never be taken too seriously. After all, it's not brain surgery. Like everything else about design, once broken down and simplified, decorating can be a joy.

The psychology of color

In 1810, the first systematic study of color on the human psyche occurred with Goethe's 'Theory of Colors'. This was followed by several other studies by noted philosophers such as Ewald Hering and Sir Isaac Newton. Since then, color analysis has been a passionate topic among philosophers and designers.

Individual colors are believed to have different affects on mood and energy. Red for example is a color that represents fire and ignites passion, action and energy. It is also considered auspicious in many cultures.

Blue on the other hand is considered calming, serene and peaceful. Green is a color of balance and growth, while yellow and oranges are optimistic and bright.

Select the best color scheme for your home

Before selecting a color scheme for your home, purchase a **color wheel** from an art supply or paint supply store to arm yourself with a basic understanding of how colors work in the scheme of each other. Color wheels are great reference tools to keep you on the right track as they show the relationship between primary, secondary and complementary colors. Colors opposite each other on the color wheel are considered complementary. One side of the wheel contains colors that are cool, and the other side displays warm colors.

Don't rely on paint chips from the hardware store to determine your choice – you need at least 1 x 1 yard (3 x 3 meters) in a patch on your walls. Preferably paint every wall in the room to give you an accurate reading of the color. You should check it in varying light conditions throughout the day as the changing light will change the color dramatically. Natural daylight will show the color in its truest form. Artificial incandescent lighting brings out warm tones, and fluorescent lighting is most unflattering, casting a blue tone over the room.

A safe and simple **rule of thumb** when selecting a color scheme is the 60:30:10 rule: 60 per cent of the room should be the dominant color, 30 per cent should be a secondary color, while the remaining 10 per cent should be the accent color.

The entire mood of a room depends on its color so think about the feeling you want to impart through the hues used. Do you want the room to feel soothing and calm or dramatic and social?

You want to get it right before purchasing an entire house worth of paint. By testing hues in large patches on the walls in question you will avoid costly mistakes. If you are using deep or vivid colors, you may wish to use large pieces of poster board, taping them to the wall, rather than painting directly onto the wall. This way you won't have to add extra layers of paint to cover the test patches once you've decided on your final color.

In **children's rooms** you can be more playful with color, but be careful not to use too many intensely loud colors and patterns that can over-stimulate them at bed time. Very bright surroundings can lead to irritability and unrest. Choose mid tones of happy colors rather than bright shades.

Feature walls of one dominant color have fallen out of favor in recent times, and if you love a color enough then you should have the confidence to paint the room in its entirety. Perhaps tone the look down by choosing a lighter value of the color if you are using it in the whole room.

All white rooms can be stunning, but be aware that they can also look stark and cold when white is used on all surfaces. If you want a light, bright room, consider a slightly warmer and deeper saturation of the neutral that you were going for to add depth to the room. The end result will look luminous and interesting rather than cold. You can also add interest by introducing texture and pattern in furniture and fabrics in the room that will look fresh against all white. Differing paint finishes in the room will also add interest, so you could paint all trims a high gloss to contrast against matte walls.

Likewise, any single color in one room can be given added punch by varying the **paint finishes**. You could use a flat wall paint, but the same color on trims in a double strength satin or gloss finish to avoid a boring room If you have too much of the same color throughout a room, you can give it life by adding embellishments such as piping, tassels, cord, fringe or gimp in a complementary color.

Paint types

Most paint sold today is **water based.** It has less VOCs (volatile organic compounds) than traditional oil-based paint that has been thought to be dangerous to the environment as well as human health. **Oil-based paints** are still sold, however. Traditionally used on trims, they can also be good for high wear areas such as floors.

Paint is available in a range of **finishes,** the most popular being **low sheen, matte, gloss, semi gloss and satin.** Low sheen is mostly used on walls and gives a standard, velvety finish. Matte has a more industrial finish and can be used in a variety of applications including furniture and is great at hiding imperfections. Gloss is, as

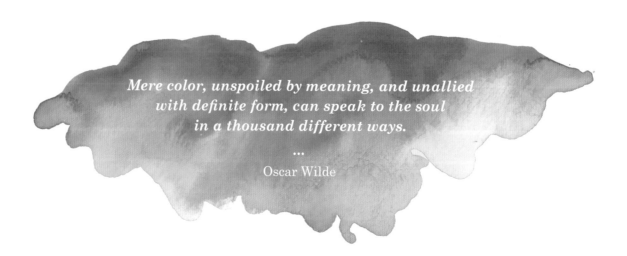

Mere color, unspoiled by meaning, and unallied with definite form, can speak to the soul in a thousand different ways.

...

Oscar Wilde

its name suggests, a high shine finish that works well on trims, window frames and doors. Satin is slightly reflective and works well in kitchens and bathrooms as it is easy to wipe clean. However, it also shows up more imperfections so is not ideal on walls that are not even and smooth underneath.

Special effect paints can be purchased from certain paint companies specializing in special effects that can add drama to a room instantly. Chalk paint, gilt paint, suede, mineral and metal finishes, lime washes, French washes and aged patinas are all options that can add that all important wow factor to your home.

Ceiling paint is traditionally white but be adventurous and think about using a color on your ceiling instead. Gloss paint looks fantastic on a ceiling as it reflects light into the room. Similarly, tinted ceilings can add instant wow factor. I have seen a room with a brushed pale silver ceiling and glossy duck egg blue walls that was utterly fabulous because it was so unexpected.

If certain rooms of your home are visible from adjacent rooms and hallways, it's important to consider how the color in each area will look in context with each other. **Create a flow** by using colors that are complementary to each other.

The right paint brush

With various widths, handles, and fibers available, to get a professional finish, it's imperative to apply the paint with the correct paint brush. Spend time researching before you embark on your painting exercise.

Paint brush types include synthetic filament heads, which are cheaper, and 100 per cent pure bristle brushes, which are best for oil-based paints. If you are painting entire walls, you will need a roller and a brush for 'cutting in' around the edges. Cheaper is not always best as a quality brush will mean you will get a smoother application, as well as waste less paint.

No-fail color combinations

Standing with hundreds of colors in front of you on a paint board in your local paint shop or hardware store can be daunting – where do you start? Color is so important in a home and it's easy to become overwhelmed and just go with all white.

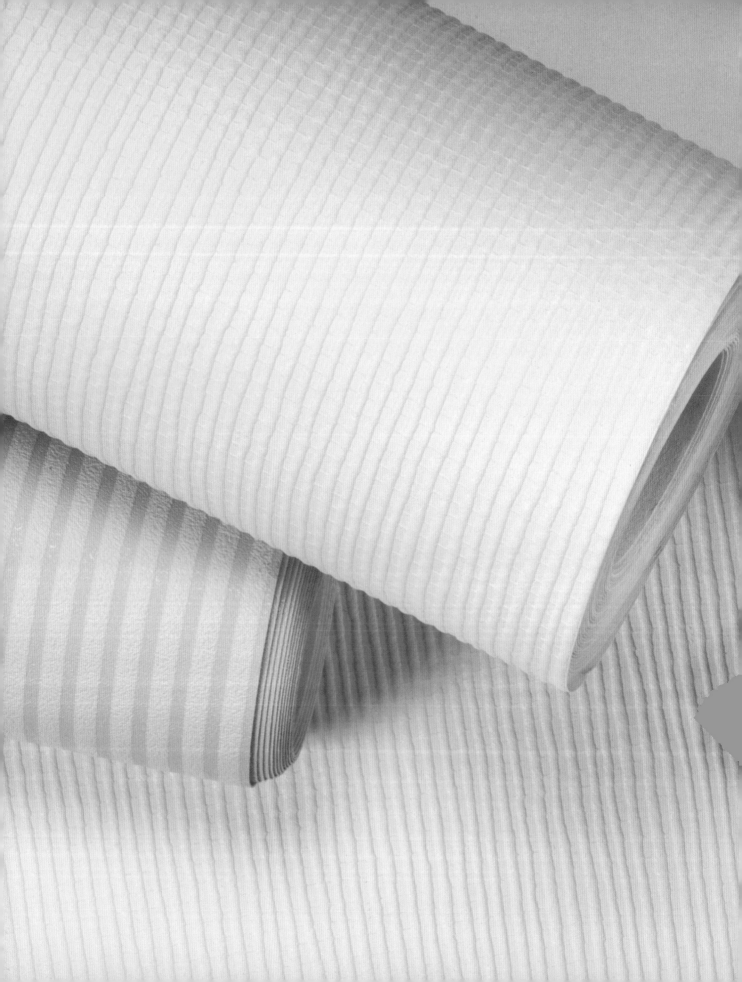

If you want to be a little more daring, here are some color combinations that are timeless and sophisticated – you can't get wrong! Think about these in terms of the entire scheme including décor and accessories, not just paint colors.

Navy, white, sand and red is classic and chic. Navy and white are often seen in nautical schemes or coastal homes. Stripes lend themselves to this look, so consider striped accessories such as cushions. Introduce beige to soften the look through décor such as timber furniture or flooring (reminiscent of sand on the beach), and a splash of red for a punch of attitude.

Black and white or charcoal and white are high contrast combinations that will always make an impact. This combination looks fantastic with a small splash of color that you can add through accessories, and easily update as your taste changes. Hot pink, orange or green all look great with black and white. You don't have to go with the strongest shade of black, consider softer shades like charcoal or a more muted grey for a less-dominant tone.

Pink and green sit opposite each other on the color wheel and are 'complementary' colors, which make for a striking effect. Due to their position on the color wheel, the combination appears more intense than if you were to select colors closer together on the wheel, creating a more visually arresting look. Gorgeous in a little girl's room, the addition of green will avoid the look of being all too pink. Pink and green were a favorite color scheme of Marie Antoinette's and were used at the Palace of Versailles.

Yellow and grey are a seemingly unusual combination however, yellow and grey work beautifully together. A hit of yellow gives a grey room the sunshine and life that it needs. Soft shades of both colors looks very pretty, or you can strengthen one color and use a softer hue in the other for more punch in the room.

White on white is an option when all else fails. The reason this is a popular choice is that white always make a space look fresh and new. If you want to use white, but avoid the space being boring, add interest by adding spashes of color, textures in soft furnishings and furniture, and by introducing varying neutral tones such a browns, caramels or beige. Choose a warm white rather than a cool blue-based white as your main color as the blue undertones will make the room look too stark.

Use texture and pattern to great effect

Pattern clashing fabrics are all the rage, but there is a definite art to executing this look successfully. With patterns, the trick to combining seemingly clashing designs is to unify them with similar tints and tones in your color scheme.

In furniture, rather than a room full of the same textures and finishes, mix glossy or lacquered pieces with rattan or other rough surfaces to create balance. As with patterns, help the differing styles to co-exist harmoniously in the room by grounding them with a **unified color scheme.**

Texture plays an enormous role in giving a room its 'feel'. Leather mixed with sisal is strong and masculine. Ruffles and velvet, on the other hand, lend a more feminine feel, so consider these elements when selecting your fabrics and textures.

Rather than a plain painted wall, why not try color blocks, stripes, or an 'effect' such as a distressed antique patina such as you'd see in an ageing European villa?

An otherwise traditional room can be given a hint of personality by **introducing a pattern** such as an animal print. Animal prints can be difficult to work with as you have to get the balance right. Be careful that you don't have too much – an entire sofa upholstered in leopard will be too dominant. The best animal prints are those that are of a high quality in both design and fabric weight.

Using a **wallpaper,** or even pretty gift wrapping paper, to line the back of open shelves is a nice way to introduce pattern into a space without it being too dominant.

Chapter 9

WINDOW FRAMES AND TREATMENTS

In my view, no space without natural light is worthy of human occupation.

John Saladino, Architectural and interior designer

Windows allow natural light to flood into your home, which is essential for a happy environment. Humans crave light – a beautiful, light-filled room has a positive affect on your psyche.

Types of window frames

Before you consider window treatments, you need to assess your current windows to determine whether the frame or the opening itself could do with an update. Often it's not difficult to update older style windows (which tend to be smaller) to larger ones that will allow more ventilation and light into your home. Also consider adding windows where there are none.

Some prevalent styles include **French windows** that usually have two panes of glass opening outwards, with shutters on the exterior. **Awning windows** have one section of glass, usually divided into two or four pieces that are pushed out so they do not require space on the inside of the home.

Inline sliding windows are also popular in modern or smaller homes as they slide on a track so that no part has to intrude on the room. These can have panels that slide, or fixed sections with just one or two moving parts.

Louvre windows are practical as they feature sections of glass that allow you to adjust the amount of air and light entering the room.

Sash windows are more old fashioned and come with a host of issues such as 'sticking' which makes them difficult to open and close if they've been re-painted over the years.

You can also have a **picture window,** which is a single panel, in various shapes and sizes that doesn't open.

Freshen up **window frames with gloss** or **semi-gloss paint**. If you want to add pizazz to the room, consider decorative molding around window frames.

Hanging options

To get the most out of your windows you will need to select the right treatment for them. The appearance of curtains and blinds are significant in an interior environment for a variety of reasons.

Firstly, they **add to the general ambiance** in a room from a decorative point of view as they pack a punch with stylish fabrics that enhance your decor. Along with the type of window, the type of window treatment you choose will determine **how much light enters the room.**

Furthermore, window coverings are essential for **privacy**. You don't want a bare window that voyeuristic neighbors can see straight through. In bathrooms, in particular, you might want to consider frosted or stained glass for discretion. Sheer curtains, usually made from a light semi-translucent woven fabric, can be useful to allow light in, but prevent visibility from outside.

Fashionable window treatment options include **shutters** and **French windows,** although more upmarket looks such as these come with a matching price tag due to their materials and finish. Poly resin shutters are a great idea in wet areas such as bathrooms and kitchens as they are made from a synthetic material that is low maintenance yet looks like more traditional timber.

For more affordable ideas, **try ready-made** tab top or eyelet curtains that can be hung directly onto a curtain rod. If you're on a budget, stick to glossy white poles, otherwise a metallic such as chrome looks modern depending on your décor and color scheme. **Decorative rods and finials** (the decorative ornamental part that sits at the end of the rod) are readily available and easy to put up, even for the most inexperienced DIYer. Curtains can be held back with matching **tie backs** that sit at each end of the curtain, and are attached to the wall.

If you're not handy with a sewing machine, the good news is that **ready-made curtains and blinds** now come in a range of choices. There are a variety of shapes, colors, fabrics, and sizes so it's likely that you will find one that suits your requirement.

It's a good idea to spend a little more and get a good quality fabric that has been treated for mold and mildew resistance, plus has a good fireproof rating.

Curtains or drapes that are made from a heavier fabric can also assist with noise absorption and insulation of hot and cold air, which is worth considering depending on the climate where you live.

During the day, open up windows to allow in fresh air and light. Draw curtains back, or pull blinds up, to allow maximum natural light to enter. This will help to improve the feel of the room.

Motorized blinds are popular in new, modern homes as they are now more affordable than ever and allow you to easily adjust the light and minimize glare entering your home. You can even control them from a remote, or if you want to really impress your friends, from your smart phone or tablet device.

Pelmets are also stylish. Tie them in with your fabric selection for a cohesive look.

In **bedrooms,** it's vital that the room can be sufficiently darkened for sleep. For this reason, curtains or blinds that have a 'blockout' lining are best to prevent morning sunlight from streaming in.

Simplicity is the ultimate form of sophistication.

...

Leonardo da Vinci

Chapter 10

Flooring

Flooring is a background to your furniture.

Anna Merotto, Canadian interior designer

Flooring makes up such a large part of the room spatially, and its treatment is a very important decision in your overall scheme.

Choosing the right flooring

It is usually best to decide on your choice of flooring first as the foundation for your design, or to leave it to your last decision to complete your overall scheme and to complement the other elements in the room. Whichever way you go, there are a number of things to consider.

Foot traffic

With so many options, it's wise to investigate the pros and cons of different variations in flooring, and it's very important to consider how your home is used and how much foot traffic it sees before you make a decision.

If you have children or pets, flooring that is practical and easy to clean is best. If you are an empty nester you will have more freedom to choose a pale wool carpet or an expensive and elaborate Persian rug.

Acoustics

Flooring can have an effect on how sound bounces around the room, so consider the impact your choice of flooring will have on the acoustics in your home.

Hard flooring creates more noise, soft flooring such as carpet absorbs sound and softens noises. However, you can reduce and break up the hard, flat surfaces in a room by adding soft objects.

Color

A dark floor will impact the light in the room in a similar way to paint and furniture choices, so be aware that flooring color choices will also affect the mood and look you create in the room. Patterned, speckled or highly textured weaves are best in high traffic areas such as children's rooms as they will better conceal any marks.

Check ratings
Carpets and rugs are now rated, so carefully check the **specifications** on the ones you are considering for its **durability** and **performance**.

Wool versus a synthetic carpet, for example, will have very different qualities in terms of use, cleaning and longevity. A good quality wool carpet that has been installed properly with underlay, scotch guarding and regular cleaning can last 10 to 20 years.

With proper maintenance, synthetic carpet can last up to 10 years before it starts to become frayed and stained. It all depends upon how you look after your carpet. Regular cleaning and maintenance will certainly help extend the life of your investment.

Wool carpets can sometimes 'shed' so be sure to ask your flooring supplier about this before you install a wool carpet to ensure that the one you've chosen won't lose fibers.

Factor in climate
Environmental factors such as heat and humidity should be considered before making a decision about your flooring. Carpet is best in cooler climes (unless you install under floor heating), and timber flooring should be avoided if you live in an area with high humidity as the moisture will affect the boards – making them expand and contract, becoming uneven.

Under-floor heating is something that you will need to put in prior to the installation of your floor.

Allergies and asthma
Hard flooring is an excellent option for those with allergies and asthma as carpets will always be a source of dust and dirt no matter how often you clean them.

Soft flooring and rugs

The beauty of modern technological advances is that soft flooring is now much more hard wearing than in previous years, meaning that carpets and rugs last longer because the fibers are easier to keep clean and won't wear down as easily.

Cut pile

A more luxurious and formal look than other styles, cut pile is created by cutting across the top of the looped yarn that results in an upright and smooth finish. While it might be more deluxe, it is also less practical as it will show more footprints, and other marks (from vacuum cleaners for example) due to its level appearance, making it a more appropriate choice for low traffic areas such as bedrooms.

Loop pile

Loop pile is made by looping the yarn to create a multitude of patterns by alternating the height and size of the loops. It looks more like natural flooring such as sisal than cut pile, which has an overall more even finish. Modern synthetic loop piles are extremely practical as they will withstand heavy traffic and won't mark easily.

Combination cut and loop pile

As its name suggests, by mixing both cut and loop pile in the one carpet you can achieve many different textures, patterns and effects such as circles, squares or rectangles. This makes the carpet more wearable as marks and stains are harder to see.

Sisal

One of my favorite types of soft flooring is sisal, a natural flooring made from the beautiful agave plant that is hard wearing and stylish. It is harder under foot but is also harder wearing. It looks great in a variety of different interior schemes, from beachy to a more formal, classic look.

Rugs

Rugs are similar to carpets in that they come in many different styles and fabrications, but the beauty of them is that you can have fun with pattern, color and texture without having to commit to wall to wall carpet, meaning you can change it with greater ease as you see fit. Usually placed over a hard surface, rugs can also be inlaid into a specific area of the floor so that they are flush with the rest of the flooring, which is a smart look. Rugs can also be placed over a neutral carpet.

A pattern over a pattern will generally be too busy and hard on the eye. Select a rug that complements the rest of your scheme by picking up on colors or textures that are already present. Rugs are also great to brighten an area with a pop of color, making a chic statement.

Hard Flooring

Hard flooring is a popular option for good reason – it's hard wearing and suitable in a variety of climates. It's cool under foot in summer and can warm the house in winter with under-floor heating. Blur the line between inside and out and make your home feel more spacious by using the same hard flooring throughout. Timber and natural stones such as travertine or limestone are good choices. Innovative new materials that are composites of stone mixed with man made materials are also good options as they are slip and frost resistant and therefore ideal for transitional spaces.

Timber

One of the most popular flooring choices, timber is a natural choice that is both practical and beautiful. Often found underneath carpets in older homes, existing timber flooring can be sanded, stained and polished in a multitude of traditional colors from light to dark, as well as specialty finishes such as white washing.

Painting timber flooring a color has become popular with the emergence of harder-wearing paint. However, be aware that this will not last as long as traditional stains.

You can lay new timber flooring directly over the top of old flooring if your floors are level, saving you time and money. Hardwood flooring from sustainable timber is the best option. The species of wood will also have an affect on the stain used. For example, pine stained black will look different to spotted gum stained black so use testers to get the color exactly right.

Floating timber

It's no surprise that floating timber floors are increasing in popularity as they are quick to install and have excellent soundproofing qualities. They can be laid directly over existing flooring such as concrete and are relatively easy to install, usually with a tongue and groove system that easily clicks together.

With the use of a foam insulation blanket underneath, floating flooring has great soundproofing qualities so the room will be less noisy than if you were to lay a traditional timber floor.

Parquetry

Featuring a pattern in the timber, and therefore more expensive than other options, parquetry flooring offers a classic, sophisticated look. Parquetry flooring can be set onto a flat, solid foundation and can be purchased in pre-assembled tiles or panels.

Bamboo

An excellent option in hard flooring because of its eco-friendly environmental sustainability – bamboo is a renewable resource as is timber – it is also extremely durability. Bamboo flooring looks modern, and is easy to install.

Tiles

Usually reserved for bathrooms and other wet areas, tiles have gone out of favor in living areas as they are cold and smaller tiles are difficult to clean due to the amount of grout between them.

Tiles come in a variety of materials from natural stone to man-made tiles. They are fantastic from a design point of view as there are so many options available with patterns and design, from mosaic to borders, hand painted to textured tiles.

If you are laying tiles you will need a solid, level surface underneath. I'd recommend get a professional tiler to lay your tiles, however, there are plenty of YouTube videos on how to do this if you want to do it yourself.

Tiles can be a slippery surface so this needs to be considered if you have small children or anyone elderly living in your home.

Polished concrete

Once limited to industrial spaces, polished concrete is now seen in more glamorous homes. It can be tailored to your needs in a variety of colors and the polished finished is light reflective and easy to clean. It's also an affordable flooring option so it's worthwhile considering.

The details are not the details.
They make the design.

...

Charles Eames, Architect and
Furniture Designer

Chapter 11

The Designer Edge

Good dressing is largely a question of detail and accessories.

Elsie de Wolfe, American actress, interior decorator and author

of 1913 book, *The House in Good Taste*

Top secrets of interior stylists

As with dressing yourself, dressing a room comes down to the finer details. The excellence exists in the combination of each component. As they say, 'the details are not the details, they are the design'.

Bring your rooms to life with carefully selected accessories and trims. The smallest objects can often make the biggest impression. But remember, the best rooms are not those that are full of 'things'. Edit well, and refine the space by making every object count. And incorporate each factor into the design through complementary textures, tones and styles.

Not everything has to match

Some of the most stylish rooms in the world aren't perfectly coordinated. In fact, often it's the opposite. An eclectic mix is much more exciting visually so be adventurous and try a few items that you wouldn't naturally assume go together. Create a 'story' by placing items together that might be different styles, but have something about them that is similar – a touch of gold paint, or an interesting shade of fuchsia in the detail of separate items is enough to tie pieces together.

Think big

When you're talking décor and accessories, big is generally better. It just says 'luxury'. A few carefully selected large-scale items make a room seem more substantial. Lots of little items tend to look cluttered and get lost among the mess.

Wallpaper in unexpected places

Wallpaper looks brilliant in small spaces – in an entry foyer, hallway, at the back of open bookshelves or cupboards, and even on the ceiling. Don't just stick to traditional patterned wallpaper either; modern textured wallpaper can look fabulous too.

If you can't afford to wallpaper an entire room, use wallpaper on a panel of the wall, or use a covered canvas as an artwork. Lining the back of open shelving with wallpaper, and even the exterior of closet doors, will inject some unexpected visual excitement into a room.

Accessorize

Nothing is worse than a home that is void of personality. Accessories help to give your home character, and a finished, designer look. Work in odd numbers for the most pleasing affect on the eye. Items such as rugs, artwork, trays and candles will all make a designer statement. Play with texture in fabrics such as leather and velvet.

Collections en masse are always a stylish statement. Display collections of cherished finds from travels or other endeavors but remember, as always, to be ruthless when 'editing' accessories. Grouping similar objects of the things that you love into collections is an effective way of styling – just be sure that they are artfully arranged.

Create opulence with plump cushions and full curtains

Designer cushions always look plump. To achieve this look, use an insert that is a couple of inches larger than the size of your cushion cover for cushions that will never look flat and cheap. Similarly, curtains that are twice or two and half times wider than the window or opening will look much fuller than curtains that just reach the distance between each end of the rod. A decorative pelmet will also make your décor seem more considered.

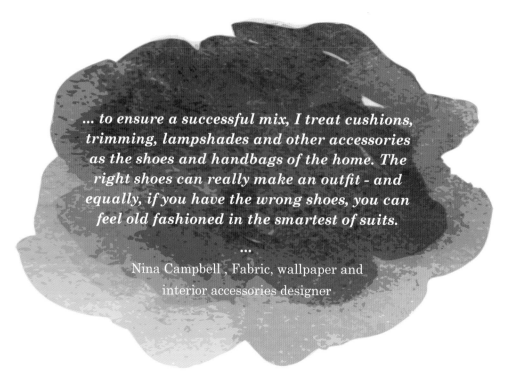

... to ensure a successful mix, I treat cushions, trimming, lampshades and other accessories as the shoes and handbags of the home. The right shoes can really make an outfit - and equally, if you have the wrong shoes, you can feel old fashioned in the smartest of suits.

...

Nina Campbell , Fabric, wallpaper and interior accessories designer

The finishing touches

These are classic statement accessories such as white linens and towels, candles, fresh flowers and silver trays. They are smart and stylish. You can't beat fresh white bed linen on beds, and white towels in the bathroom. Far from impractical, they are easy to bleach when necessary and always look crisp.

Building layers in your décor through details such as piping, flanges, skirts, valances, pelmets, and monograms will also give you a successful designer look. Think about monogramming some plain white hand towels in your bathroom with your initials to give your home an air of grace and elegance.

Fashionable architectural features

Features such as decorative moldings – crown moldings, beveled panels, grooved posts and fluted slat details – will all give your home a stately and sophisticated look. Classic details such as these can be given a modern look by pairing them with an appropriate paint scheme and contemporary accessories.

Art

Art is the finishing touch that gives a room its definition. Think outside the square – a mixture of vintage plates, oversized exotic doors from locations such as Morocco or Indonesia, or children's artworks from daycare or school are all interesting options.

Mirrored walls

Mirrored walls are one of the ultimate features in elegant interiors. They hark back to a day when homes were a showpiece. Just cover one wall in a main room of your home to avoid it feeling like you're at an amusement park, and consider an interesting finish such as an aged mirror to give your room some depth and avoid it being too showy and dominant.

Cladding, paneling and pressed tin

Adding textured panels to your walls can give your home an added dimension that takes it out of the ordinary. Whitewashed timber cladding looks gorgeous in beach houses, and old-fashioned pressed tin, which is both affordable and easy to install, has had a resurgence in recent times.

How you display your art is almost as important as the actual art itself. It can be hung in a collection (as in a gallery), leant up against the wall atop a table, or if large enough it can be leant against a wall on the floor.

The framing is also as significant as the subject matter, so invest in good quality framing that will last and also enhance the artworks beautifully.

House plants

House plants are brilliant as they have the ability to enhance your interior environment by absorbing harmful air pollutants. Think of them as the prettiest air purifiers around! They are lovely to have around the home and are a much better option than faux flowers or plants that attract dust and never look chic.

It's very important to select the right plants and care for them appropriately. Make sure you place them in places with the right amount of lighting, and water them as instructed by your local garden shop.

Here are some plants that will thrive indoors and enhance the décor of your home.
- Madonna or peace lily
- Fiddle leaf fig tree
- Snake plants
- Ferns
- Spider plants
- Philodendrons
- Pothos
- English ivy
- Miniature bamboo

If in doubt, talk to your landscaper or visit your local garden shop for advice.

When it came to style, Coco Chanel knew what she was talking about. Your interior should be layered with personality and tell your story. This is the secret of how the best designers produce the finest interiors.

Designer tips for styling your coffee table

Many of the best interior stylists will tell you that a stylish coffee table vignette with on-trend accents is **essential in the most chic abodes.** For this reason, it is important to give this piece of furniture some closer attention.

Start by considering your existing coffee table – is it the correct **proportions** for your room, and the furniture it will sit alongside? If not, invest in a new one. If it will still work but needs a **makeover,** a splash of fun metallic paint on the legs or base, or **a new glass or marble top** will work wonders to improve its looks.

It doesn't have to be transparent glass – a smoky gray that is semi-transparent can look very sophisticated in the right room. A mirrored finish or a polished natural stone is also chic.

If you go for a different look – timber perhaps – consider a distressed finish , which is very practical for coffee tables in houses with kids or animals. A distressed or weathered finish conceals a multitude of bumps and scratches, and can enhance the aged finish – the more lived in, the better.

Lay an interesting **rug** under your coffee table and then start to compile your accessories atop the table. **Collections of items** look good when placed together, and an obvious choice is a group of stylish books.

Add interest with other **ornaments,** and play with texture and detail. If your table is timber, a glass ornament – vintage ashtray, vase or simply a decorative item **–** will look great. Next add an element from **nature** – a beautiful mossy rock, some flowers in the vase, a succulent or other plant – anything petite and with an architectural or interesting shape work best.

Then you'll want to add some **color** – anything that gives the table punch and interest. Metallics are also great if you're sticking to a more neutral palette. A **candle** is the finishing touch that will also add a pleasant aroma when you are entertaining guests.

However, **don't overcrowd the table** but use your discretion and your eye to determine the right amount of objects to create a pleasing scene. Also don't place anything on the surface that is too tall, and out of proportion with everything else. Low objects work best.

The beautiful thing about displays such as coffee table settings is that they can be **changed regularly** so that you won't get bored with one look.

A final word

Decorating your home can truly be a project from which you gain great satisfaction. By breaking each element down into achievable tasks, you can take it step by step and reduce the unwanted stress that is usually associated with renovating or redecorating.

Find inspiration in the world around you, develop your mood board for your overall plan and for each room you plan to decorate. Work within your budget but most of all, have fun.

The best homes are those that are layered over time, so don't feel rushed and enjoy the process. Nothing is permanent so you can always change parts or all of your décor as the season, or your taste, changes.

Happy decorating!

Juliet xxx

Acknowledgements

There are many people whom I would like to thank. Firstly to my husband, Charlie Albone, the father of my children and the love of my life – I could not have done this book without your love and support. You are so talented, have an amazing eye for design, and are a constant source of inspiration. You also make me laugh every day. Thank you for being my best friend.

My children, Leo and Hartford, you are my greatest joy, and my greatest blessing. There are no words to describe my love for you and I am always here for you.

My father, Colin Love, you are my best mate and my hero. I could not love you more. I am so grateful and proud to be your daughter. I don't know a more devoted father and don't know what I would do without you.

My mother, Angela Belle McSweeney, my angel and my constant support, I am eternally grateful for your love and your always inspirational advice. You always believe in me, and always back me up. We're in this together.

To my amazing mother-in-law Sue Albone, thank you for coming to my rescue time and again, and to Liz, Ben, Tim, Victoria and Daphne, thank you for being so caring and supportive. I am lucky to call you all my family. To the wonderful Diane Ward at New Holland, thank you for providing me with this opportunity and for your support. You have made a dream come true.

To the brilliant Brooke Evrard, you are the most fabulous photographer; I have loved working with you on this book. Producing each image with you has been a joy and I thank you for your endless enthusiasm, professionalism and patience. I look forward to seeing your career go from strength to strength.

To my amazing best friends, Lucie McGeoch, Kate McFadyen Jasmine Stone, Phoebe Barter and Lauren Prince, thank you for your endless support and encouragement, and for always being there for me. Friends like you are one in a million and I'm very lucky to call you my mates. And finally, to God, thank you for my blessings.

Photo credits

Juliet Love – pp. 10, 14, 16, 21, 35, 38, 72, 114

Brooke Evrard – Front Cover, Back Cover, pp. 2, 6, 12, 22, 23, 26, 28, 31, 42, 44, 45, 49, 50, 62, 66, 69, 70, 73, 76, 77, 79, 80, 82, 83, 84, 87, 90–91, 92, 95, 96, 98,100, 101, 103, 104, 105, 106, 107, 108, 109, 110, 111, 116, 118, 120, 121, 122, 125, 126, 127, 129, 140, 161, 174, 179, 183, 186, 188, 189

Emma Blomfield – Urban Road Designer Rug Collection, Photography by Suzie Atken for pp. 64, 97

Melissa Hockley, HeadFirst Scribbles – p. 58

Fotolia – pp. 18, 19, 52, 53, 54, 55, 56, 112, 115, 130, 134, 136, 143, 144, 148–149, 151, 152, 154, 166

Shutterstock – pp. 33, 36, 38, 41, 46, 60, 62, 63, 88, 130, 133, 136 ,157, 158, 162, 165, 168, 171, 172, 176, 184

First published in 2015 by New Holland Publishers Pty Ltd
London • Sydney • Auckland

The Chandlery Unit 009 50 Westminster Bridge Road London SE1 7QY United Kingdom
1/66 Gibbes Street Chatswood NSW 2067 Australia
5/39 Woodside Ave Northcote, Auckland 0627 New Zealand

www.newhollandpublishers.com

A record of this book is held at the British Library and the National Library of Australia.

ISBN 9781742576398

Managing Director: Fiona Schultz
Publisher: Diane Ward
Project Editor: Susie Stevens
Designer: Lorena Susak
Proofreader: Jessica McNamara
Production Director: Olga Dementiev

Printer: Toppan Leefung Printing Limited

10 9 8 7 6 5 4 3 2 1

Keep up with New Holland Publishers on Facebook
www.facebook.com/NewHollandPublishers